Azrah Kamala Shashi

Delightful Thai Food

Celebrity Chefs' Cookbooks

Azrah Kamala Shashi
Delightful Thai Food

TIMES EDITIONS

Delightful Thai Food

Chef: **Azrah Kamala Shashi**
Chef's Assistant: **Anne Rozario**
Vegetable and Fruit Carving: **Mohd Fadzil Ismail**

Project Editor/Editor of the Malay Edition: **Jamilah Mohd Hassan**
Art Director/Designer: **Tuck Loong**
Photographer: **Jenhor Siow**
Editor of the English Edition: **Bina P. Batlivala**
Translator: **Wee Lee Lian**
Project Co-ordinator: **Christine Chong**
Production Manager: **Anthoney Chua**

The publisher wishes to thank **Metrojaya Berhad**, Malaysia; **The Mines Beach Resort and SPA**, Malaysia; **Mr Steven Ng of Ming Court Vista Hotel**, Malaysia, and **Ms Assila Emir** for the loan of their crockery and utensils.

Published by Times Editions
An imprint of Times Media Private Limited
A member of the Times Publishing Group

Times Centre, 1 New Industrial Road
Singapore 536196
Tel: (65) 284 8844   Fax: (65) 285 4871
E-mail: te@tpl.com.sg
Online Book Store: http://www.timesone.com.sg/te

Times Subang
Lot 46, Subang Hi-Tech Industrial Park
Batu Tiga, 40000 Shah Alam
Selangor Darul Ehsan, Malaysia
Tel & Fax: (603) 736 3517
E-mail: cchong@tpg.com.my

Printed by KHL Printing Co Pte Ltd, Singapore

ISBN 981 232 122 5

For my dearest husband, S. Shashitharan

Contents

Thai food, with its exotic blend of flavours and styles has become increasing popular in many countries. Thai restaurants can be found in most metropolitan cities around the globe. It would soon be apparent to anyone with a discerning palate, that Thai cuisine has a regional slant. Thai food is a blend of Chinese, Malay, Indian, Myanmar, Khmer, Laotian and to a lesser extent, Portuguese cuisines. Yet, Thai food has maintained its own distinct identity, it is a harmonious blend of indigenous spices and products and multi-cultural influences.

Thailand is divided into four regions: North, Northeast, Central and South. The cuisine of the North region was influenced by its neighbours—Myanmar and Laos. Pork is used extensively, glutinous rice is preferred and coconut milk is not as widely used as in the South.

The Northeast also known as Isan, is the poorest of the four regions. The cuisine reflects the influence of Laos. It ranges from the strangely exotic—grasshoppers and snails can be found on many a menu, to the popular Kao Man Som Tam Malakor (Unripe Papaya Salad) and Haw Mok Pla (Thai Fish Paste in Banana Leaf Casing).

In Bangkok, the cosmopolitan city of the central region, gourmets can enjoy 'palace cuisine'. The highest quality of fruits, vegetables and rice from all the regions are available here. There is a lot of Chinese influence as evidenced by the ubiquitous noodle stalls.

In the South, Thailand is bordered by Malaysia and is home to most of its Muslim minority. The influence of Indian and Malay cuisine is evidenced in the use of spices, coconut milk and chillies. Indian style Gaeng Mussaman Kai (Chicken Mussaman Curry) and Malay influenced Tom Yam Goong are examples of this influence. It is also interesting to note that unlike the North and Northeast regions where herbs play a premier role in seasoning and taste, the 'stronger' spices are used in the South.

My love of Thai food began many years ago. I was introduced to the rudiments of Thai cooking in Bangkok more than twenty years ago. This book has been designed with you, the dear reader, in mind. The recipes range from the simple to the delightful and will provide you with many wonderful experiences in the kitchen.

My teacher emphasised then, as I do now, that while exact measurements might help the beginner, experience and individual taste decide the final product. In this book, seasonings like salt, sugar, lime juice and chillies were measured according to my taste. Please adjust them to suit your preferences. Measurements have been provided in Metric, Imperial and American systems to facilitate chefs in different parts of the world.

Traditionally, chillies and other spices were ground into a powder or a paste with mortar and pestle. For the convenience-oriented cook, an electric coffee grinder or food processor will achieve the same results. Use what you are comfortable with.

Pork is used extensively in Thailand, especially in the North, Northeast and Central regions. In this book, I have not used pork in the recipes. However, readers may substitute any recipe that calls for meat, with pork.

I would like to thank my friends and family for their tremendous help and encouragement. I especially want to thank my husband, Shashitharan, whose inspiration made this book possible.

Steamed Curry Rice with Vegetable Pickles

Rice Dish | 15-minute Preparation | 45-minute Cooking | Serves 4

Ingredients

180 ml | 6 fl oz | 3/4 cup cooking oil

500 grams | 1 pound, 1 1/2 ounces chicken fillet, cut into 2.5-cm | 1-inch pieces

1 tablespoon meat curry powder

4 dried Chinese mushrooms, soaked in hot water, drained and quartered

225 grams | 8 ounces | 1 cup long-grain rice, washed and drained

6 shallots, peeled and sliced

2 tomatoes, cut in wedges

2 cardamoms

1 cm | 1/2 inch cinnamon stick

375 ml | 12 fl oz | 1 1/2 cups chicken stock (refer to page 78)

carved radish

Vegetable Pickles*

Finely Ground Paste

8 cloves garlic, peeled

2 tablespoons preserved soy bean paste (tau jiew nam)

1 cm | 1/2 inch young ginger, peeled

Method

1. Heat the cooking oil and sauté the finely ground paste until fragrant.
2. Add the chicken, meat curry powder, mushrooms, rice and shallots and stir-fry until the liquid has been absorbed. Transfer into a bowl or a flat-bottomed casserole and add the tomatoes, cardamoms, cinnamon and chicken stock and mix well.
3. Steam over rapidly boiling water for about 30 minutes or until the rice is cooked.
4. Garnish with radish and serve with Vegetable Pickles.

Chef's note: The curry rice may be cooked in a rice cooker instead of being steamed.

*Vegetable Pickles

125 ml | 4 fl oz | 1/2 cup vinegar

250 grams | 9 ounces | 1 1/8 cups sugar

1 tablespoon salt

1 large cucumber, peeled, quartered lengthways then sliced

5 shallots, peeled and sliced

3 red chillies, seeded and finely sliced

3 sprigs coriander leaves (cilantro), cut into 1-cm | 1/2-inch lengths

Method

1. Combine the vinegar, sugar and salt.
2. Add the cucumber, shallots and chillies and toss well.
3. Soak for about 30 minutes. Garnish with coriander leaves (cilantro).

Gaeng Khun Som
(Sour and Hot Marrow Curry)

Vegetable Dish | 15-minute Preparation | 30-minute Cooking | Serves 6

Ingredients

1 portion thin coconut milk (refer to page 78)

1 kilogram | 2 pounds, 3 ounces chicken, cut into small pieces

1 portion boiled coconut cream (refer to page 78)

60 ml | 2 fl oz | 1/4 cup fish sauce (nam pla)

350 grams | 12 1/2 ounces marrows (large zucchini), peeled, quartered lengthways then cut into 5-cm | 2-inch lengths

100 grams | 3 1/2 ounces coriander leaves (cilantro), cut into 1-cm | 1/2-inch lengths

red chilli strips

crisp-fried shallots

Finely Ground Paste

15 dried chillies, seeded, soaked in hot water and drained

8 shallots, peeled

8 cloves garlic, peeled

1 stalk lemon grass, finely sliced

10 white peppercorns

1 teaspoon salt

5 cm | 2 inches galangal, peeled

2 coriander roots

2.5 cm | 1 inch dried shrimp paste

2 tablespoons crushed palm sugar (jaggery) or brown sugar

110 grams | 4 ounces dried salted sole fish, fried and coarsely pounded

Method

1. Bring the thin coconut milk to a boil, add the chicken and simmer for 15 minutes.
2. Heat the boiled coconut cream for 5 minutes and stir-fry the finely ground paste until fragrant.
3. Add the fish sauce and marrows (large zucchini) and continue to stir-fry until the vegetable is tender.
4. Add the chicken along with the gravy and simmer for about 10 minutes.
5. Garnish with coriander leaves (cilantro), red chilli strips and crisp-fried shallots before serving.

(Clockwise from top left) Vegetable Pickles, Steamed Curry Rice, Gaeng Khun Som (Sour and Hot Marrow Curry).

Gaengom Mara
(Fish Curry with Bitter Gourd)

Main Dish | 15-minute Preparation |
30-minute Cooking | Serves 6

Ingredients

- 1 portion boiled coconut cream
  (refer to page 78)
- 1/2 portion red curry paste
  (*Nam Prik Gaeng Ped*, page 78)
- 60 ml | 2 fl oz | 1/4 cup fish sauce
  (*nam pla*)
- 2 tablespoons crushed palm sugar
  (jaggery) or brown sugar
- 1 portion thin coconut milk
  (refer to page 78)
- 700 grams | 1 1/2 pounds catfish, cleaned
  and cut into 5-cm | 2-inch pieces
- 500 grams | 1 pound, 1 1/2 ounces bitter
  gourd, halved lengthways, seeded,
  finely sliced and soaked in salt water
- 2 spring onions (scallions), cut into
  1-cm | 1/2-inch lengths

Method

1. Heat the boiled coconut cream for 5
   minutes and stir-fry the red curry
   paste for 10 minutes or until
   fragrant.
2. Add the fish sauce, palm sugar
   (jaggery) or brown sugar and the
   thin coconut milk and cook for 5
   minutes.
3. Add the catfish and bitter gourd and
   continue to cook for another 5–8
   minutes.
4. Garnish with spring onions
   (scallions) before serving.

Pan Klip
(Savoury Steamed Dumplings)

Side Dish | 30-minute Preparation |
30-minute Cooking | Serves 4

Ingredients

- 125 grams | 4 1/2 ounces | 1 cup rice flour,
  sifted
- 60 grams | 2 ounces | 1/2 cup tapioca
  flour, sifted
- 60 grams | 2 ounces | 1/2 cup arrowroot
  flour, sifted
- 250 ml | 8 fl oz | 1 cup water
- Chicken Filling*
- banana leaves
- 1 tablespoon vegetable oil
- 4 lettuce leaves, sliced
- 3 cloves garlic, peeled, finely chopped
  and fried until golden brown
- 2 red chillies, seeded and finely chopped

Method

1. Combine the rice flour, tapioca flour,
   arrowroot flour and water and mix
   well.
2. Cook over medium heat, stirring
   constantly, until it thickens. Remove
   from heat and set aside to cool.
3. Divide the flour mixture into small
   balls of dough about 3.5 cm |
   1 1/2 inches in diameter. Cover with a
   damp cloth.
4. Flatten a ball of dough into a thin
   sheet and place 1 heaped teaspoon of
   Chicken Filling on top. Wrap the
   sheet around the filling and pinch
   into a half-moon shape. Repeat until
   all the ingredients are used up.
5. Line a steamer with the banana
   leaves brushed with vegetable oil and
   place the dumplings on top. Steam
   over rapidly boiling water for 8
   minutes.
6. Serve on a dish lined with lettuce
   leaves. Garnish with the fried garlic
   and red chillies.

*Chicken Filling

- 3 1/2 tablespoons cooking oil
- 250 grams | 9 ounces chicken fillet,
  finely diced
- 1 large onion, peeled and finely diced
- 3 tablespoons fish sauce (*nam pla*)
- 3 tablespoons sugar
- 1 tablespoon crushed palm sugar
  (jaggery) or brown sugar
- 70 grams | 2 1/2 ounces | 1/2 cup ground,
  roasted peanuts

Finely Ground Paste

- 3 cloves garlic, peeled
- 1 cm | 1/2 inch galangal, peeled
- 1 teaspoon white peppercorns

Method

1. Heat the cooking oil and sauté the
   finely ground paste until fragrant.
2. Add the chicken, onion, fish sauce,
   sugar and palm sugar (jaggery) or
   brown sugar.
3. Add the peanuts and mix well. Set
   aside.

Chef's note: The dumplings may be served with
chilli sauce.

(Clockwise from top left) Chilli sauce, Gaengom Mara (Fish Curry with Bitter Gourd), Pan Klip (Savoury Steamed Dumplings).

Pad Thai Sai Khai
(Thai Fried Rice Noodles)

Noodle Dish | 20-minute Preparation |
15-minute Cooking | Serves 4

Ingredients

90 ml | 3 fl oz | 3/8 cup cooking oil

3 cloves garlic, peeled and finely chopped

4 shallots, peeled and finely chopped

300 grams | 10 1/2 ounces Thai flat rice noodles, soaked in water for 10 minutes and drained

250 ml | 8 fl oz | 1 cup water

2 cloves garlic, peeled and sliced

140 grams | 5 ounces squid, cleaned and sliced

50 grams | 1 2/3 ounces chicken fillet, sliced

50 grams | 1 2/3 ounces preserved radish (hua chai po), sliced

1 piece bean curd, deep-fried, cut into 2 then sliced

1 tablespoon powdered chilli

3 tablespoons fish sauce (nam pla)

3 eggs, beaten, fried into thin omelettes and cut into strips, save some for garnishing

50 grams | 1 2/3 ounces Chinese chives, cut into 2.5-cm | 1-inch lengths + some for garnishing

1 tablespoon light soy sauce

500 grams | 1 pound, 1 1/2 ounces bean sprouts, tailed

roasted peanuts

Method

1. Heat 3 tablespoons cooking oil and sauté the chopped garlic and shallots until light brown.
2. Add the rice noodles and 125 ml / 4 fl oz / 1/2 cup water. Stir constantly to keep the noodles from sticking together, cook until half-done. Set aside.
3. Heat the remaining cooking oil, stir-fry the garlic slices, squid, chicken, preserved radish, bean curd, powdered chilli and fish sauce for 5 minutes or until fragrant.
4. Add the noodles and continue to stir-fry. Pour in the remaining water and stir well. Add omelette strips, Chinese chives, light soy sauce and half of the bean sprouts. Stir-fry for 5 minutes.
5. Garnish with remaining omelette strips, Chinese chives and bean sprouts, and peanuts before serving.

Chef's note: *Kway teow* noodles can be substituted for Thai rice noodles.

Kai Thod Kratian Prik
(Thai Fried Chicken Wings)

Main Dish | 15-minute Preparation |
30-minute Cooking | Serves 6

Ingredients

12 chicken wings

1.25 litres | 40 fl oz | 5 cups cooking oil

Marinade (blended)

3 coriander roots, finely ground

3 cloves garlic, peeled and finely ground

1 teaspoon ground white pepper

1 1/2 teaspoon salt

3 tablespoons fish sauce (nam pla)

1 teaspoon dark soy sauce

1 teaspoon monosodium glutamate

1 tablespoon crushed palm sugar (jaggery) or brown sugar

Dipping Sauce (blended)

60 ml | 2 fl oz | 1/4 cup lime juice

60 grams | 2 ounces | 1/4 cup sugar

4 shallots, peeled and thinly sliced

60 ml | 2 fl oz | 1/4 cup fish sauce (nam pla)

1 tablespoon powdered chilli

1 tablespoon crushed palm sugar (jaggery) or brown sugar

Method

1. Rub the chicken wings with the marinade and leave in the refrigerator for 6 hours.
2. Heat the cooking oil and deep-fry about 6 chicken wings at a time for 2–3 minutes. Drain.
3. Serve with Dipping Sauce.

Chef's note: The longer the chicken is marinated the more flavourful it is. At a minimum, it should be marinated for at least one hour.
    The dipping sauce can also be used to season fish prior to barbecuing.

(Clockwise from top left) Dipping Sauce, Kai Thod Kratian Prik (Thai Fried Chicken Wings), Pad Thai Sai Khai (Thai Fried Rice Noodles).

Coconut Cream Seafood Soup

Soup Dish | 30-minute Preparation | 60-minute Cooking | Serves 4

Ingredients

375 ml | 12 fl oz | 1¹/₂ cups water

450 grams | 1 pound | 4¹/₂ cups grated, peeled coconut

110 grams | 4 ounces squid, cleaned and cut into 1-cm | ¹/₂-inch rings

110 grams | 4 ounces small prawns (shrimps), shelled with tail intact

1 medium-sized flower crab, quartered

2 stalks lemon grass, sliced

4 kaffir lime leaves

4 coriander roots

1 litre | 32 fl oz | 4 cups chicken stock (refer to page 78)

2 tablespoons cooking oil

6 shallots, peeled and sliced

3 cloves garlic, peeled and chopped

2.5 cm | 1 inch galangal, peeled and sliced

200 grams | 7 ounces pea eggplants

4 red chillies, seeded and sliced

1 tablespoon crushed palm sugar (jaggery) or brown sugar

2 tablespoons sesame oil

Marinade (blended)

2 tablespoons fish sauce (*nam pla*)

2 tablespoons light soy sauce

2 tablespoons thick tamarind juice, extracted from 55 grams | 2 ounces tamarind pulp and 2 tablespoons water

1 teaspoon powdered turmeric

Method

1. Add the water to the grated coconut and extract 500 ml / 16 fl oz / 2 cups coconut milk. Keep aside.
2. Marinate the squid, prawns (shrimps) and crab for 5–10 minutes.
3. Pound (or blend in an electric food processor) the lemon grass, kaffir lime leaves and coriander roots until fine. Transfer to a large saucepan.
4. Add the chicken stock, bring to a boil, then reduce the heat and simmer for 30 minutes. Strain and reserve the stock.
5. Heat the cooking oil and fry the shallots, garlic, galangal, pea eggplants and red chillies until fragrant. Remove and add to the chicken stock.
6. Add the coconut milk, boil for 20 minutes on low heat, stirring constantly to avoid curdling.
7. Add the marinated seafood along with the marinade and palm sugar (jaggery) or brown sugar and cook for 8 minutes.
8. Drizzle with sesame oil before serving.

Chef's note: You can garnish this soup with chopped coriander leaves (cilantro).

Pla Prio Wan

(Fried Fish with Mushroom Ginger Sauce)

Main Dish | 15-minute Preparation | 30-minute Cooking | Serves 4

Ingredients

500 grams | 1 pound, 1¹/₂ ounces black pomfret, cleaned and gutted

500 ml | 16 fl oz | 2 cups cooking oil

Mushroom Ginger Sauce*

2 red chillies, seeded and cut into strips

1 spring onion (scallion), cut into 2.5-cm | 1-inch lengths

Batter (blended)

85 grams | 3 ounces | ³/₄ cup plain (all-purpose) flour, sifted

1¹/₄ teaspoons salt

1¹/₂ tablespoons corn oil

125 ml | 4 fl oz | ¹/₂ cup water

Method

1. Make diagonal slashes in a lattice pattern on both sides of the fish.
2. Coat the fish with batter and deep-fry until golden brown. Set aside on a serving plate.
3. Pour the Mushroom Ginger Sauce over the fish.
4. Garnish with chilli strips and spring onions (scallions).

Chef's note: The fish can also be garnished with chopped coriander leaves (cilantro).

*Mushroom Ginger Sauce

6 dried Chinese mushrooms, soaked in hot water, drained and thinly sliced

60 ml | 2 fl oz | ¹/₄ cup vinegar

2 tablespoons light soy sauce

60 grams | 2 ounces | ¹/₄ cup sugar

85 ml | 2¹/₂ fl oz | ¹/₃ cup water

60 grams | 2 ounces pickled ginger, cut into thin strips

1 tablespoon cornflour (cornstarch), mixed with 2 tablespoons water

Method

Combine all the sauce ingredients and cook for 5 minutes. Thicken the sauce with the cornflour (cornstarch) mixture.

(From top) Pla Prio Wan (Fried Fish with Mushroom Ginger Sauce), Coconut Cream Seafood Soup.

Pap Pak Ruam Mit
(Stir-fried Mixed Vegetables)

Vegetable Dish | 20-minute Preparation |
8-minute Cooking | Serves 6

Ingredients

- 3 tablespoons cooking oil
- 3 cloves garlic, peeled and chopped
- 1 small red capsicum (bell pepper), seeded and cut into chunks
- 120 grams | 4 1/2 ounces mange tout (snow peas)
- 120 grams | 4 1/2 ounces baby corn cobs
- 120 grams | 4 1/2 ounces cauliflower florets
- 120 grams | 4 1/2 ounces broccoli florets
- 85 grams | 3 ounces canned button mushrooms
- 2 tablespoons crushed palm sugar (jaggery) or brown sugar
- 1 tablespoon light soy sauce
- 1 tablespoon fish sauce (nam pla)
- 3 bird's eye chillies, cut into thin rounds

Method

1. Heat the cooking oil and sauté the garlic until fragrant.
2. Add the vegetables and stir-fry for 1 minute.
3. Mix the palm sugar (jaggery) or brown sugar with soy sauce, fish sauce and bird's eye chillies and add to the vegetables. Cook until the vegetables are crisp.

Chef's note: Stir-frying the vegetables helps retain the freshness and texture, they remain crisp and colourful.
   This vegetable dish can be served with Prik Dong Sauce*.

*Prik Dong Sauce

- 8 red chillies, sliced diagonally
- 3 shallots, peeled and sliced
- 90 ml | 3 fl oz | 3/8 cup vinegar
- 3 tablespoons sugar
- 1/2 teaspoon salt
- 1 teaspoon chopped sweet basil leaves (bai horapa)

Method

Mix all the ingredients until well blended.

Gaeng Panaeng Nu-Ea
(Red Curry Beef)

Main Dish | 20-minute Preparation |
20-minute Cooking | Serves 4–6

Ingredients

- 1 portion thin coconut milk (refer to page 78)
- 1 kilogram | 2 pounds, 3 ounces beef fillet (tenderloin), cut into small pieces
- 1 portion boiled coconut cream (refer to page 78)
- 1 portion red curry paste (Nam Prik Gaeng Ped, page 78)
- 60 ml | 2 fl oz | 1/4 cup fish sauce (nam pla)
- 2 tablespoons crushed palm sugar (jaggery) or brown sugar
- 280 grams | 10 ounces | 2 1/3 cups pounded, roasted peanuts
- 1/2 teaspoon kaffir lime rind slices
- 3 red chillies, halved lengthways
- 5 green chillies, halved lengthways
- 2 sprigs sweet basil leaves (bai horapa)

Method

1. Cook thin coconut milk and the beef over medium heat until the meat is tender.
2. Heat the boiled coconut cream for 5 minutes and stir-fry the red curry paste until fragrant and oil floats on top.
3. Add the cooked beef along with the coconut milk, fish sauce, palm sugar (jaggery) or brown sugar, peanuts, kaffir lime rind and stir well. Add the red chillies, green chillies and sweet basil leaves.

Chef's note: Serve this dish with hot rice. The beef may be substituted with chicken or pork.

(From top) Gaeng Panaeng Nu-Ea (Red Curry Beef), Pap Pak Ruam Mit (Stir-fried Mixed Vegetables).

Steamed Fish a'la Thai

Main Dish | 10-minute Preparation |
35-minute Cooking | Serves 4

Ingredients

280 grams | 10 ounces fish bones or
    1 cube anchovy stock

2.5 cm | 1 inch galangal, peeled and
    thinly sliced

60 ml | 2 fl oz | 1/4 cup fish sauce
    (*nam pla*)

200 grams | 7 ounces sliced cabbage

1 medium carrot, peeled and cut into
    thin strips

280 grams | 10 ounces pickled vegetables
    (*kieam chai*), cut into small strips

1 large tomato, quartered

2 stalks lemon grass, cut into 2.5-cm |
    1-inch lengths

3 kaffir lime leaves

1 litre | 32 fl oz | 4 cups water

sugar

juice of 1 lime

2 large red chillies, thinly sliced

2 sour plums, diced

5 cm | 2 inches ginger, peeled and cut
    into thin strips

2 tablespoons cooking oil

2–3 shiitake mushrooms, soaked in hot
    water, drained and cut into strips

1 (500 grams | 1 pound, 1 1/2 ounces) sea
    bass or garoupa, cleaned and gutted

2 sprigs coriander leaves (cilantro), cut
    into 1.25-cm | 1/2-inch lengths

1 red chilli, cut into thin strips

Method

1. To make the soup, boil fish bones or
   anchovy cube, half of the galangal
   slices, 2 tablespoons fish sauce,
   cabbage, carrot, pickled vegetables,
   tomato, lemon grass and kaffir lime
   leaves in water for 15–20 minutes.
   Season with sugar and lime juice.
   Set aside.
2. Combine chilli slices, sour plums,
   ginger strips, remaining galangal
   slices and mushroom strips. Sprinkle
   half the mixture onto a heatproof
   dish and place the fish on top.
   Sprinkle the remainder on top of the
   fish along with remaining fish sauce.
3. Steam fish for 10–15 minutes over
   rapidly boiling water.
4. To serve, pour the boiled soup on the
   fish, garnish with coriander leaves
   (cilantro) and red chilli strips.

Chef's note: After steaming the fish, discard the
stock as it has a strong fishy odour.
    As a variation, the fish can be steamed
together with soaked rice vermicelli and 180 ml /
6 fl oz / 3/4 cup chicken stock. The vermicelli
acquires a unique taste.
    You can also add crisp-fried shallots as
garnishing and drizzle the dish with 1
tablespoons of oil from frying these shallots.

Kao Cluk Nam Prik
(Tossed Rice in Chilli Paste)

Rice Dish | 30-minute Preparation |
20-minute Cooking | Serves 4

Ingredients

250 grams | 9 ounces | 1 1/4 cups long-
    grain rice, washed and drained

375 ml | 12 fl oz | 1 1/2 cups water

3 tablespoons fish sauce (*nam pla*)

2 tablespoons crushed palm sugar
    (jaggery) or brown sugar

150 ml | 5 fl oz | 5/8 cup lemon or lime
    juice

250 grams | 9 ounces beef fillet
    (tenderloin), boiled for 10 minutes
    or until tender, then cut into thin
    strips

300 grams | 10 1/2 ounces chicken breast,
    boiled for 5 minutes or until tender,
    then finely shredded

Finely Ground Paste

15 cloves garlic, peeled

12 bird's eye chillies

150 grams | 5 1/2 ounces | 1 cup dried
    prawns (shrimps), soaked in water
    and drained

180 grams | 6 1/4 ounces | 3/4 cup crushed,
    roasted shrimp paste

Method

1. Combine the rice and water, and
   cook in a rice cooker. Fluff the rice
   and set aside to cool.
2. Combine the fish sauce, palm sugar
   (jaggery) or brown sugar, lemon or
   lime juice with the finely ground
   paste and mix into a sauce.
3. Mix rice and sauce thoroughly. Add
   half of the beef and chicken to the
   rice mixture and mix well.
4. Serve rice on a serving plate and top
   with the remaining beef and chicken.

Chef's note: This dish may be garnished with
carrot, cucumber and coriander leaves (cilantro).

(From top right) Kao Cluk Nam Prik (Tossed Rice in Chilli Paste), Steamed Fish a'la Thai.

Rume Olah Tieng
(Beef Cutlets Wrapped in Egg Net)

Side Dish | 15-minute Preparation |
30-minute Cooking | Serves 4

Ingredients

350 grams | 12½ ounces minced
   (ground) beef

100 grams | 3½ ounces minced
   (ground), shelled prawns (shrimps)

90 ml | 3 fl oz | ⅜ cup cooking oil

1 large onion, peeled and finely diced

1 tablespoon minced (ground), peeled
   garlic

70 grams | 2½ ounces | ½ cup ground,
   roasted peanuts

1 tablespoon chopped coriander roots

1 teaspoon ground white pepper

3 tablespoons fish sauce (nam pla)

1 tablespoon sugar

6 eggs, beaten

1 sprig coriander leaves (cilantro),
   stalk removed

1 red chilli, seeded and cut into thin
   strips

1 cucumber, peeled and sliced

1 spring onions (scallions)

carrot, carved into flower shape

Method

1. Combine the beef and prawns
   (shrimps) and mix well.
2. Heat 60 ml / 2 fl oz | ¼ cup cooking
   oil and sauté the onion and garlic.
   Add the beef and prawns (shrimp)
   mixture and stir-fry until slightly dry.
3. Add the peanuts, coriander roots,
   white pepper, fish sauce and sugar.
   Fry until the meat is slightly dry. Set
   aside.
4. Heat some of the remaining cooking
   oil and sprinkle the egg by hand in
   criss-cross lines to resemble a net,
   approximately 10 cm / 4 inches in
   diameter. Continue until all the egg
   is used up.

5. To assemble each cutlet, put a few
   coriander leaves (cilantro) and red
   chilli strips on each egg circle. Top
   with 1 heaped tablespoon of the
   cooked beef and prawns (shrimps)
   mixture and wrap the egg to form a
   square. Continue with the remaining
   ingredients.
6. Serve garnished with cucumber,
   spring onions (scallions) and carrot.

Chef's note: Chicken or pork may be used instead
of beef.
   A laced pancake (roti jala) mould can be used
to make the net.

Rice Vermicelli Salad

Salad Dish | 25-minute Preparation | Serves 6

Ingredients

210 grams | 7½ ounces small prawns
   (shrimps)

juice of 6–7 limes

125 grams | 4½ ounces shallots, peeled
   and finely sliced

60 grams | 2 ounces coriander leaves
   (cilantro), chopped

4 cloves garlic, peeled and chopped

85 ml | 2½ fl oz | ⅓ cup fish sauce
   (nam pla)

3 stalks Chinese chives, cut into
   0.5-cm | ¼-inch lengths

10 bird's eye chillies, finely sliced

70 grams | 2½ ounces | ⅓ cup sugar

500 grams | 1 pound, 1½ ounces
   bean sprouts, tailed, blanched
   and drained

5 cm | 2 inches dried shrimp paste,
   toasted and coarsely ground

800 grams | 1¾ pounds rice vermicelli,
   blanched and drained

2 red chillies, cut into thin rounds

Method

1. Blanch the prawns (shrimps) in hot
   water. Shell, devein and halve
   lengthways.
2. Combine prawns (shrimps) with
   lime juice, shallots, coriander leaves
   (cilantro), garlic, fish sauce, Chinese
   chives, chillies, sugar and bean
   sprouts. Mix well.
3. Add the shrimp paste and rice
   vermicelli. Toss the mixture until
   well blended.
4. Garnish with red chillies.

Chef's note: Rice vermicelli can be substituted
with glass noodles (woon sen).
   To enhance the flavour, add 250 grams /
9 ounces / 2½ cups roasted, grated, peeled
coconut before serving. You can also add hard-
boiled eggs as garnishing.

(From top) Rice Vermicelli Salad, Rume Olah Tieng (Beef Cutlets Wrapped in Egg Net).

Grilled (Broiled) Spring Chicken

Main Dish | 10-minute Preparation |
30-minute Cooking | Serves 4

Ingredients

- 2 tablespoons cooking oil
- 4 cloves garlic, peeled and chopped
- 1 large onion, peeled and cut into small wedges
- 2 (450 grams | 1 pound each) spring chickens, cleaned and halved
- radish, carved into flower shape
- carrot, carved into leaf shape

Sauce (blended)

- 2 tablespoons vinegar
- 2 tablespoons chilli sauce
- 1 tablespoon Lea & Perrins sauce
- 180 ml | 6 fl oz | 3/4 cup tomato sauce
- 2 tablespoons fish sauce (*nam pla*)
- 60 ml | 2 fl oz | 1/4 cup fresh pineapple juice
- 1 tablespoon oyster sauce
- 2 tablespoons lime juice

Method

1. Heat the cooking oil, fry the garlic and onions until fragrant.
2. Add the sauce ingredients and cook for 5 minutes. Remove from heat and cool.
3. Coat the chicken with the sauce and grill (broil) for 15–20 minutes until well done.
4. Serve garnished with radish and carrot.

Chef's note: Chicken may be substituted with lamb chops for a variation.
   This sauce is versatile, it can be prepared one day ahead. It can also be used as a marinade for meat.

Gaeng Mussaman Kai

(Chicken Mussaman Curry)

Main Dish | 20-minute Preparation |
25-minute Cooking | Serves 4

Ingredients

- 100 grams | 3 1/2 ounces tamarind pulp
- 3 tablespoons water
- 2 bay leaves
- 2.5 cm | 1 inch cinnamon stick
- 2 cardamoms
- 1 portion thin coconut milk (refer to page 78)
- 1 kilogram | 2 pounds, 3 ounces chicken, cut into small pieces
- 2 tablespoons fish sauce (*nam pla*)
- 1 portion boiled coconut cream (refer to page 78)
- 1 portion Mussaman curry paste (*Nam Prik Gaeng Mussaman*, page 78)
- 2 tablespoons ground, roasted peanuts
- 3 tablespoons crushed palm sugar (jaggery) or brown sugar
- 6 shallots, peeled and sliced
- 2 large potatoes, boiled, peeled and quartered
- 2 sprigs sweet basil leaves (*bai horapa*), stalks removed
- 1 red chilli, seeded and chopped

Method

1. Combine the tamarind pulp and water and extract the juice. Set aside.
2. Pan-fry the bay leaves, cinnamon and cardamoms. Set aside.
3. Pour the thin coconut milk over the chicken, add fish sauce and cook until tender.
4. Heat the boiled coconut cream for 5 minutes and stir-fry the Mussaman curry paste until fragrant.
5. Add the chicken along with the coconut milk. Add peanuts, palm sugar (jaggery) or brown sugar and tamarind juice.
6. Add the pan-fried spices, shallots and potatoes and simmer for 15 minutes.
7. Garnish with sweet basil leaves and chopped chilli.

Chef's note: Beef may be used instead of chicken. An additional 750 ml / 24 fl oz / 3 cups of thin coconut milk will be required to cook the beef.

(From top) Grilled (Broiled) Spring Chicken, Gaeng Mussaman Kai (Chicken Mussaman Curry).

Kai Tung Na Tung
(Chicken Coconut Curry)

Main Dish | 15-minute Preparation |
25-minute Cooking | Serves 6

Ingredients

55 grams | 2 ounces tamarind pulp

60 ml | 2 fl oz | 1/4 cup water

1 portion thin coconut milk
(refer to page 78)

450 grams | 1 pound chicken, cut into
small pieces

300 grams | 10 1/2 ounces shelled and
deveined prawns (shrimps)

6 shallots, peeled and finely ground

7 cloves garlic, peeled and finely ground

3 tablespoons crushed palm sugar
(jaggery) or brown sugar

1 coriander root, finely chopped

90 ml | 3 fl oz | 3/8 cup fish sauce (nam pla)

10 white peppercorns

1 portion boiled coconut cream
(refer to page 78)

125 grams | 4 1/2 ounces | 2/3 cup roasted
peanuts, coarsely pounded

100 grams | 3 1/2 ounces coriander leaves
(cilantro), cut into 1-cm | 1/2-inch
lengths

2 red chillies, seeded, cut into thin strips
and soaked in cold water

spring onions (scallions)

Method

1. Combine the tamarind pulp and
water to extract the juice. Set aside.
2. Cook the thin coconut milk with the
chicken, prawns (shrimps), shallots,
garlic, palm sugar (jaggery) or brown
sugar, coriander root, fish sauce,
white peppercorns and tamarind
juice until the chicken is tender.
3. Heat the boiled coconut cream in a
separate pan for 5 minutes. Add to
the chicken.
4. Add the peanuts and mix well.
5. Garnish with coriander leaves
(cilantro), spring onions (scallions)
and red chilli strips before serving.

Chef's note: Beef or pork may be substituted for
chicken.
    This dish may be served with fried rice
crackers and assorted raw vegetables.

Seafood and Egg Parcel

Main Dish | 30-minutes Preparation |
15-minute Cooking | Serves 6

Ingredients

1 tablespoon cooking oil

4 eggs, beaten

Seafood Filling*

1 red chilli, cut into thin strips

lettuce

Method

1. Heat the cooking oil in a frying pan
(skillet) and pour in the eggs to make
an omelette. Spoon the Seafood
Filling in the centre of the omelette.
Fold opposite sides of the omelette,
first the top and the bottom, then the
right and the left sides to make a
neat square parcel. Slide out on to a
serving plate, folded side down.
2. Make two slits on top and open up to
make it look like a flower.
3. Garnish with red chilli and lettuce.
Serve hot.

*Seafood Filling

2 tablespoons cooking oil

200 grams | 7 ounces red snapper fillet,
diced

200 grams | 7 ounces squid, cleaned and
cut into rings

200 grams | 7 ounces medium tiger
prawns (shrimps), shelled, deveined
and diced

2 dried Chinese mushrooms, soaked in
water and diced

100 grams | 3 1/2 ounces | 3/4 cup
green peas

2 tablespoons fish sauce (nam pla)

1 teaspoon cornflour (cornstarch),
blended with 1 tablespoon water

1 sprig coriander leaves (cilantro),
chopped

Finely Ground Paste

4 shallots, peeled

3 cloves garlic, peeled

4 coriander roots

1/2 teaspoon finely sliced kaffir lime rind

1/2 teaspoon black peppercorns

Method

1. Heat the cooking oil and sauté the
finely ground paste until fragrant.
2. Add the fish, squid, prawns
(shrimps), mushrooms, green peas
and stir-fry for 3 minutes.
3. Add the fish sauce and stir well.
Thicken the filling with the cornflour
(cornstarch) mixture. Stir in
coriander leaves. Remove from heat
and set aside.

(From top) Seafood and Egg Parcel, Kai Tung Na Tung (Chicken Coconut Curry).

Mee Katy
(Thai Style Fried Rice Vermicelli)

Noodle Dish | 20-minute Preparation |
25-minute Cooking | Serve 6

Ingredients

- 2 portions boiled coconut cream (refer to page 78)
- 10 shallots, peeled and finely pounded
- 3 tablespoons preserved soy bean paste (*tau jiew nam*)
- 1 teaspoon ground white pepper
- 2 tablespoons sugar
- 2 tablespoons lemon or lime juice
- 3 tablespoons fish sauce (*nam pla*)
- 3 pieces bean curd, cut into two, then sliced into 1-cm | 1/2-inch pieces
- 250 grams | 9 ounces small shelled prawns (shrimps)
- 400 grams | 14 ounces rice vermicelli, blanched and drained
- 200 grams | 7 ounces Chinese chives, cut into 2.5-cm | 1-inch lengths + extra for garnishing
- 250 grams | 9 ounces bean sprouts, tailed
- 2 red chillies, seeded and finely sliced
- 2 eggs, beaten, fried into thin omelettes and cut into strips

Method

1. Heat the boiled coconut cream for 5 minutes. Add the shallots, preserved soy bean paste, pepper, sugar, lemon or lime juice and fish sauce. Stir-fry until fragrant.
2. Add the bean curd and prawns (shrimps), and mix well before adding the rice vermicelli, Chinese chives and bean sprouts.
3. Garnish with Chinese chives, red chilli and omelette strips.

Chef's note: One sprig oriander leaves (cilantro), cut into 1-cm / 1/2-inch lengths can also be added, if desired.

Batter Fried Sea Mussels with Egg

Side Dish | 15-minute Preparation |
15-minute Cooking | Serves 6

Ingredients

- 140 grams | 5 ounces | 1 cup tapioca flour, sifted
- 70 grams | 2 1/2 ounces | 1/2 cup plain (all-purpose) flour, sifted
- 375 ml | 12 fl oz | 1 1/2 cups water
- 250 grams | 9 ounces shelled, cooked mussels
- 60 ml | 2 fl oz | 1/4 cup cooking oil
- 30 grams | 1 ounce | 3/8 cup sliced, fried garlic
- 6 eggs
- 90 ml | 3 fl oz | 3/8 cup fish sauce (*nam pla*)
- 90 grams | 3 1/4 ounces | 3/8 cup sugar
- 300 grams | 10 1/2 ounces bean sprouts, tailed
- 2 sprigs coriander leaves (cilantro), cut into 2.5-cm | 1-inch lengths
- 2 spring onions (scallions), cut into 2.5-cm | 1-inch lengths

Sauce (blended)

- 3 red chillies, finely sliced
- 1 tablespoon sugar
- 1 teaspoon salt
- 125 ml | 4 fl oz | 1/2 cup vinegar

Method

1. Combine the tapioca flour with plain (all-purpose) flour. Add water and mix into a batter. Divide into six portions.
2. Wash and drain the mussels and divide into six portions.
3. Heat the cooking oil and add 1 tablespoon of fried garlic, and one portion each of the mussels and the batter.
4. When the batter begins to solidify, break an egg on the top. Add 1 tablespoon of fish sauce and one teaspoon of sugar.
5. Use a spatula and slightly scramble the mixture. Then add some bean sprouts, coriander leaves (cilantro) and spring onions (scallions). Cook until evenly brown. Repeat the procedure until all the ingredients are used up.
6. Serve with the sauce.

Chef's note: Mussels can be substituted with cockles or small oysters.

(Anticlockwise from top) Batter Fried Sea Mussels with Egg, Mee Katy (Thai Style Fried Rice Vermicelli), the sauce.

French Beans in Coconut Milk

Vegetable Dish | 15-minute Preparation | 15-minute Cooking | Serves 6

Ingredients

500 grams | 1 pound, 1¹/₂ ounces French beans

2 tablespoons cooking oil

2 cloves garlic, peeled and chopped

2 stalks lemon grass, bruised and cut into four pieces

225 grams | 8 ounces small prawns (shrimps), shelled and deveined

2.5 cm | 1 inch galangal, peeled and sliced

¹/₂ teaspoon powdered turmeric

2 kaffir lime leaves + extra for garnishing

2 tablespoons fish sauce (*nam pla*)

1 teaspoon sugar

¹/₂ portion thick coconut milk (refer to page 78)

1 red chilli, seeded and chopped

Method

1. Top, tail, string and halve the French beans.
2. Heat the cooking oil and fry the garlic, lemon grass, prawns (shrimps), galangal and powdered turmeric for 5 minutes.
3. Add the French beans, kaffir lime leaves, fish sauce and sugar. Cook for 3 minutes.
4. Add the coconut milk and cook for another 3 minutes, stirring constantly to prevent the milk from curdling.
5. Serve garnished with red chilli and kaffir lime leaves.

Chef's note: French beans can be substituted with long beans or mange tout (snow) peas.

Chicken Curry with Galangal

Main Dish | 15-minute Preparation | 25-minute Cooking | Serves 4

Ingredients

1 portion thin coconut milk (refer to page 78)

200 grams | 7 ounces galangal, peeled and finely sliced

2 stalks lemon grass, slightly bruised

3 kaffir lime leaves + extra for garnishing

1 kilogram | 2 pounds, 3 ounces chicken, skinned and cut into small pieces

60 ml | 2 fl oz | ¹/₄ cup fish sauce (*nam pla*)

1 portion boiled coconut cream (refer to page 78)

juice of 3 limes

4 dried chillies, pan-fried and crushed into flakes

1 tablespoon crushed palm sugar (jaggery) or brown sugar

1 red chilli, cut into flower shape

Method

1. Boil the thin coconut milk with the galangal, lemon grass, kaffir lime leaves, chicken pieces and fish sauce until the chicken is tender. Set aside.
2. Heat the boiled coconut cream for 5 minutes in a separate pan. Add the chicken with the gravy. Stir well and simmer over low heat.
3. Add the lime juice, chilli flakes and palm sugar (jaggery) or brown sugar. Bring to a boil and cook for 2–3 minutes.
4. Garnish with kaffir lime leaves and red chilli before serving.

(From top) Chicken Curry with Galangal, French Beans in Coconut Milk.

Thai Stewed Beef

Main Dish | 10-minute Preparation |
3–4-hour Cooking | Serves 4–6

Ingredients

500 grams | 1 pound, 1 1/2 ounces beef
     shank, cut into 2.5-cm | 1-inch cubes
2.5 litres | 80 fl oz | 10 cups water
1 cm | 1/2 inch cinnamon stick
3 coriander roots
2 tablespoons light soy sauce
1 tablespoon dark soy sauce
salt
1 bay leaf
250 grams | 9 ounces lettuce or water
     convolvulus, cut into 3.5-cm |
     1 1/2-inch pieces, blanched and
     drained
90 grams | 3 ounces coriander leaves
     (cilantro), cut into 2.5-cm | 1-inch
     lengths
3 tablespoons chopped, fried garlic
1 teaspoon ground white pepper

Method

1. Put the beef into a pot. Add the
   water, cinnamon, coriander roots,
   light and dark soy sauce, salt and
   bay leaf.
2. Bring to a boil, cover and simmer
   over low heat for 3–4 hours or until
   the meat is tender.
3. Transfer to a serving dish lined with
   blanched lettuce or water
   convolvulus.
4. Garnish with coriander leaves
   (cilantro), fried garlic and pepper.
5. Serve hot with rice.

Chef's note: This dish may be cooked in a
pressure cooker. Cook the beef for 30 minutes
with 500 ml / 16 fl oz / 2 cups water. Remove
from heat and cool. Add 750 ml / 24 fl oz / 3 cups
boiled water and cook for another 15–20 minutes.
     You may also use an electric crock-pot.
Follow step 1, then allow the meat to simmer
overnight in the crock-pot.
     Beef can be substituted with pork or mutton.

Pra Thad Lom

(Wantons with Sticky Chilli Sauce)

Side Dish | 20-minute Preparation |
30-minute Cooking | Serves 4

Ingredients

10 wanton wrappers
Chicken and Prawn (Shrimp) Filling*
banana leaves
435 ml | 14 fl oz | 1 3/4 cups cooking oil
Sticky Chilli Sauce (refer to page 80)
lettuce
carrot, carved into flower shape

Method

1. Place 1 tablespoon Chicken and
   Prawn (Shrimp) Filling in the centre
   of a wanton wrapper. Bring the ends
   of the wrapper to the centre and
   secure with a piece of thread. Repeat
   until all the ingredients are used up.
2. Line a steamer with the banana
   leaves, place the wantons on top and
   steam over rapidly boiling water for
   about 10–15 minutes. Allow to cool.
3. Deep-fry the steamed wantons until
   golden brown and crisp.
4. Garnish with lettuce and carrot.
   Serve with Sticky Chilli Sauce.

*Chicken and Prawn (Shrimp) Filling

450 grams | 1 pound minced (ground)
     chicken
150 grams | 5 1/2 ounces minced
     (ground), shelled prawns (shrimps)
1 tablespoon minced (ground)
     chicken fat
1 egg, beaten
2 tablespoons fish sauce (*nam pla*)
1 tablespoon sugar
2 tablespoons cornflour (cornstarch)

Finely Ground Paste

2 cloves garlic, peeled
10 white peppercorns
1 coriander root

Method

Combine the chicken, prawns
(shrimps), chicken fat, egg, fish sauce,
sugar, cornflour (cornstarch) and the
finely ground paste and mix well into a
smooth paste.

Chef's note: Wanton wrappers can be substituted
with 2 sheets soy bean skin (*fu chok*), softened in
water and cut into 7.5-cm / 3-inch squares.

(Clockwise from top left) Chilli sauce, Thai Stewed Beef, Pra Thad Lom (Wantons with Sticky Chilli Sauce).

Gaeng Som Banjapan
(Savoury Seafood Soup)

Soup Dish | 25-minute Preparation | 20-minute Cooking | Serves 6

Ingredients

- 140 grams | 5 ounces tamarind pulp
- 1.4 litres | 45 fl oz | 5$^{1}/_{2}$ cups water
- 280 grams | 10 ounces catfish, cut into 5-cm | 2-inch pieces
- 110 grams | 4 ounces long beans, cut into 2.5-cm | 1-inch lengths
- 110 grams | 4 ounces cauliflower florets
- 110 grams | 4 ounces turnip, peeled and sliced into 0.5 cm | $^{1}/_{4}$ inch thick
- 55 grams | 2 ounces carrot, peeled and sliced into 0.5 cm | $^{1}/_{4}$ inch thick
- 110 grams | 4 ounces pickled mustard, cut into 1.5-cm | $^{3}/_{4}$-inch pieces
- 2 tablespoons crushed palm sugar (jaggery) or brown sugar
- 90 ml | 3 fl oz | $^{3}/_{8}$ cup fish sauce (*nam pla*)
- 280 grams | 10 ounces prawns (shrimps), shelled and deveined
- 110 grams | 4 ounces squids, cleaned and cut into rings
- 110 grams | 4 ounces spring onions (scallions), finely chopped

Finely Ground Paste

- 8 dried chillies, seeded, soaked in hot water and drained
- 6 shallots, peeled
- 2.5 sq cm | 1 sq inch dried shrimp paste
- 5 cloves garlic, peeled

Method

1. Combine the tamarind pulp and 90 ml / 3 fl oz / $^{3}/_{8}$ cup water and extract the juice. Set aside.
2. Boil the remaining water, add the finely ground paste and the catfish and continue to boil for about 5–10 minutes.
3. Remove the catfish and set aside to cool. Shred the fish and add to the soup.
4. Add the long beans, cauliflower, turnip, carrot, pickled mustard, palm sugar (jaggery) or brown sugar, fish sauce, prawns (shrimps), squid and tamarind juice. Boil for 5–8 minutes.
5. Serve and garnish with spring onions (scallions).

Chef's note: The fishy taste and smell from a fish is usually produced by the slime under the gills, this is especially true of catfish. Clean the slime under the gills thoroughly before cooking. Avoid stirring the fish for the first 8 minutes, when cooking as this helps further reduce the fishy aroma.

Gaeng Keo Wan Kai
(Chicken in Green Curry)

Main Dish | 20-minute Preparation | 20-minute Cooking | Serves 8

Ingredients

- 1 portion boiled coconut cream (refer to page 78)
- 1 portion green curry paste (*Nam Prik Gaeng Keo Wan*, page 78)
- 2 tablespoons crushed palm sugar (jaggery) or brown sugar
- 60 ml | 2 fl oz | $^{1}/_{4}$ cup fish sauce (*nam pla*)
- 1.5 kilograms | 3 pounds, 4$^{1}/_{2}$ ounces chicken, cut into small pieces
- 6 kaffir lime leaves
- 1 portion thin coconut milk (refer to page 78)
- 6 red chillies, cut into thin rounds
- 140 grams | 5 ounces pea eggplants
- 2 sprigs sweet basil leaves (*bai horapa*)

Method

1. Heat the boiled coconut cream for 5 minutes, add the green curry paste and stir-fry for 5 minutes or until fragrant.
2. Add the palm sugar (jaggery) or brown sugar, fish sauce, chicken pieces, kaffir lime leaves and thin coconut milk. Stir well and continue cooking for 15 minutes.
3. When the gravy is thick, add red chillies, pea eggplants and sweet basil leaves. Stir well.
4. Serve hot with steamed rice.

(From top) Gaeng Som Banjapan (Savoury Seafood Soup), Gaeng Keo Wan Kai (Chicken in Green Curry).

Savoury Golden Cups with Seafood Filling

Side Dish | 20-minute Preparation | 30-minute Cooking | Serves 4

Ingredients

6 spring roll wrappers, cut into 7.5-cm | 3-inch squares
cooking oil for brushing
Seafood Filling*

Method

1. Brush a piece of spring roll wrapper with a little cooking oil and gently press over an upturned 6.5-cm | 2½-inch fluted muffin tin.
2. Brush another piece of spring roll wrapper with cooking oil and arrange on top to form a star-shaped case. Repeat with the remaining spring roll squares.
3. Transfer the cases onto a baking tray and bake in a preheated oven at 200°C / 400°F for 12–15 minutes or until light brown and crisp. Set aside.
4. To serve, fill the baked spring roll cups with Seafood Filling.

Chef's note: You can garnish this dish with spring onions (scallions).

*Seafood Filling

150 grams | 5½ ounces squid, cleaned and finely diced
200 grams | 7 ounces tiger prawns (shrimps), shelled, deveined and finely diced
50 grams | 2 ounces crabmeat, shredded
60 ml | 2 fl oz | ¼ cup fish sauce (nam pla)
90 ml | 3 fl oz | ⅜ cup cooking oil
100 grams | 3½ ounces | ¾ cup cashew nuts, coarsely chopped
2 cloves garlic, peeled and finely chopped
1 red chilli, finely sliced
2 kaffir lime leaves, torn into halves
100 grams | 3½ ounces canned button mushrooms, finely sliced
1 tablespoon crushed palm sugar (jaggery) or brown sugar
2 teaspoons lemon or lime juice
1 tablespoon cornflour (cornstarch), blended with 2 tablespoons water

Method

1. Marinate the squid, prawns (shrimps) and crabmeat in fish sauce for 5–10 minutes.
2. Heat the cooking oil and stir-fry the cashew nuts until slightly brown. Drain and set aside.
3. In the same oil, sauté the garlic, chilli and kaffir lime leaves for 3 minutes. Add the mushrooms and marinated ingredients and stir-fry for 2–3 minutes.
4. Add the cashew nuts and mix well before adding the palm sugar (jaggery) or brown sugar and lemon or lime juice. Stir in the cornflour (cornstarch) mixture to thicken.

Phanang Kai
(Chicken Ragout)

Main Dish | 15-minute Preparation | 30-minute Cooking | Serves 6

Ingredients

250 grams | 9 ounces | 2½ cups grated coconut
625 ml | 20 fl oz | 2½ cups water
90 ml | 3 fl oz | ⅜ cup cooking oil
600 grams | 1 pound, 5 ounces chicken, cut into small pieces and seasoned with 1 teaspoon salt
4 kaffir lime leaves
2 tablespoons crushed palm sugar (jaggery) or brown sugar
2 tablespoons fish sauce (nam pla)
2 sprigs sweet basil leaves (bai horapa), stalks removed
spring onions (scallions)
carrot, carved into flower shape

Finely Ground Paste

10 shallots, peeled
10 dried chillies, seeded, soaked in hot water and drained
10 cloves garlic, peeled
2.5 cm | 1 inch galangal, peeled
1 stalk lemon grass, finely sliced
½ teaspoon chopped kaffir lime peel
1 tablespoon chopped coriander roots
10 white peppercorns
1 tablespoon salt
2.5 sq cm | 1 sq inch dried shrimp paste

Method

1. Combine the grated coconut and 125 ml / 4 fl oz / ½ cup water to extract thick coconut milk. Add another 500 ml / 16 fl oz / 2 cups water to the coconut to extract thin coconut milk. Set aside.
2. Heat 3 tablespoons cooking oil and stir-fry the chicken until slightly brown. Drain and set aside.
3. Heat the remaining cooking oil and fry the finely ground paste over low heat until fragrant and oil floats on top.
4. Add the fried chicken, kaffir lime leaves, palm sugar (jaggery) or brown sugar, fish sauce and thin coconut milk. Stir well, cover and simmer over low heat for about 20 minutes or until the chicken is tender and the gravy is thick.
5. Add the thick coconut milk and continue to cook for about 5 minutes. Add the sweet basil leaves.
6. Garnish with spring onions (scallions) and carrot and serve hot with rice.

Chef's note: Beef or pork may be used instead of chicken. Increase the thin coconut milk to 750 ml / 24 fl oz / 3 cups. Simmer the beef or pork in the thin coconut milk until tender before adding any of the other ingredients.

(From top) Phanang Kai (Chicken Ragout), Savoury Golden Cups with Seafood Filling.

Khao Mok Kai
(Thai Chicken Rice)

Rice Dish | 20-minute Preparation |
30-minute Cooking | Serves 6

Ingredients

355 grams | 12¹/₂ ounces | 1¹/₂ cups long-grain rice

625 ml | 20 fl oz | 2¹/₂ cups water

1¹/₂ teaspoons salt

1 teaspoon vinegar

60 ml | 2 fl oz | ¹/₄ cup evaporated milk

600 grams | 1 pound, 5 ounces chicken, cut into small pieces

1.5 cm | ³/₄ inch ginger, peeled and finely ground

3 cloves garlic, peeled and finely ground

125 ml | 4 fl oz | ¹/₂ cup cooking oil

70 grams | 2¹/₂ ounces | ¹/₃ cup butter

10 shallots, peeled and sliced

3 potatoes, peeled and cut into wedges

3 tablespoons saffron water, extracted from ¹/₄ teaspoon saffron strands and 3 tablespoons water

crisp-fried shallots

spring onions (scallions), chopped

1 red chilli, carved into flower shape

Spice Mixture

1 teaspoon roasted coriander seeds

¹/₂ teaspoon roasted cumin seeds

¹/₄ teaspoon powdered turmeric

¹/₄ teaspoon powdered cinnamon

2 cloves

seeds from 3 cardamoms

2 teaspoons meat curry powder

1 tablespoon powdered chilli

1 tablespoon salt

Method

1. Wash the rice, add water and salt, cook until three-quarters done.
2. Mix vinegar and evaporated milk and set aside for 5 minutes to form sour milk.
3. Marinate chicken with sour milk, ginger, garlic and ground spice mixture for 1 hour.
4. Heat the cooking oil and butter and fry the shallots until brown. Drain and set aside.
5. Fry the potato wedges and the chicken separately, in the same oil, until brown. Drain and set aside.
6. Place the partially cooked rice in a rice cooker. Arrange the fried shallots, chicken pieces and potato wedges on top. Cover the rim of the rice cooker with a tea towel and place the cooker cover on top. Cook until the rice is done.
7. Sprinkle the saffron water on the rice and mix well.
8. Garnish with crisp-fried shallots, spring onions and red chilli.

Hot and Sour Taro Leaf Stalk Curry

Vegetable Dish | 25-minute Preparation |
35-minute Cooking | Serves 4

Ingredients

55 grams | 2 ounces tamarind pulp

1.2 litres | 39 fl oz | 4⁴/₅ cups water

4 taro leaf stalks (*phueak*), peeled and cut into 5-cm | 2-inch lengths

1 teaspoon salt

1 tablespoon cooking oil

3 tablespoons fish sauce (*nam pla*)

3 tablespoons crushed palm sugar (jaggery) or brown sugar

4 kaffir lime leaves, shredded

1 dried salted sole fish, fried and finely pounded

Finely Ground Paste

1 (250 grams | 9 ounces) snakehead fish or catfish, cleaned and de-boned

4 dried chillies, seeded, soaked in hot water and drained

1 small stalk lemon grass, finely sliced

1 cm | ¹/₂ inch galangal, peeled

3 shallots, peeled

1 clove garlic, peeled

1 sq cm | ¹/₂ sq inch dried shrimp paste

¹/₂ teaspoon white peppercorns

0.5 cm | ¹/₄ inch lesser ginger (*kra chai*), peeled

Method

1. Combine the tamarind pulp and 250 ml / 8 fl oz / 1 cup water and extract the juice. Set aside.
2. Boil half of the tamarind juice with the taro leaf stalks and salt for about 10 minutes. Remove from heat and set aside.
3. Dissolve the finely ground paste in 1 litre / 32 fl oz / 4 cups water and bring to a boil.
4. Add the remaining tamarind juice, cooking oil, fish sauce, palm sugar (jaggery) or brown sugar and kaffir lime leaves. Continue to boil for 15 minutes.
5. Add the dried salted sole fish and the taro leaf stalks mixture. Boil for another 10 minutes.
6. Serve hot with rice.

Chef's note: Taro leaf stalks may be substituted with any other stem vegetable such as celery, asparagus or heart of banana stem.

(Clockwise from top right) Khao Mok Kai (Thai Chicken Rice), Hot and Sour Taro Leaf Stalk Curry, chilli sauce.

Kang Rau Punk
(Yam Puffs)

Side Dish | 20-minute Preparation |
20-minute Cooking | Serves 6

Ingredients

- 600 grams / 1 pound, 5 ounces mature yam, peeled and finely diced
- 2 tablespoons margarine
- 100 grams | 3½ ounces | ⅔ cup green pea flour (*tang mein*), sifted
- 2 tablespoons vegetable oil
- 1 teaspoon sugar
- ½ teaspoon salt
- Chicken Filling*
- 1 litre | 32 fl oz | 4 cups cooking oil
- spring onions (scallions)
- carrot, carved into leaf shape
- radish, carved into leaf shape
- red chilli, carved into flower shape
- Sweet and Sour Sauce (refer to page 80)

Method

1. Steam the yam over rapidly boiling water until tender. Mash into a smooth paste. Add the margarine, green pea flour, vegetable oil, sugar and salt. Knead into a dough. Divide the dough into equal portions.
2. Flatten a portion of dough, place 1 heaped tablespoon of Chicken Filling on top and shape to form a cylinder. Repeat until all the ingredients are used up.
3. Heat the cooking oil and deep-fry the yam puffs until golden brown.
4. Garnish with spring onions, carrot, radish and red chilli. Serve with Sweet and Sour Sauce.

*Chicken Filling

- 2 tablespoons cooking oil
- 2 cloves garlic, peeled and finely chopped
- 1 coriander root, finely chopped
- 250 grams | 9 ounces chicken fillet, finely diced
- 125 grams | 4½ ounces bamboo shoots, peeled and finely diced
- 3 dried Chinese mushrooms, soaked in hot water, drained and finely diced
- 2 teaspoons light soy sauce
- 2 tablespoons sugar
- 2 tablespoons fish sauce (*nam pla*)
- 1 teaspoon cornflour (cornstarch), blended with 2 tablespoons water

Method

1. Heat the cooking oil and sauté the garlic and coriander root until fragrant.
2. Add the chicken, bamboo shoots, mushrooms, soy sauce, sugar and fish sauce and stir-fry until all the moisture is absorbed.
3. Stir in the cornflour (cornstarch) mixture to thicken the sauce. Set aside to cool.

Chef's note: Canned bamboo shoots can be used if fresh ones are not available.

Khanom Krok
(Steamed Rice Cake with Savoury Toppings)

Side Dish | 20-minute Preparation |
20-minute Cooking | Serves 6

Ingredients

- 250 grams | 9 ounces | 1¼ cups long-grain rice, washed and drained
- 30 grams | 1 ounce | ¼ cup cooked rice
- 75 grams | 2½ ounces | ¾ cup grated, peeled coconut
- ½ teaspoon salt
- 750 ml | 24 fl oz | 3 cups hot water
- Prawn (Shrimp) Topping*
- Coconut Milk Topping**
- 1 red chilli, seeded and cut into thin strips
- 1 sprig coriander leaves (cilantro), chopped
- pumpkin, carved into flower shape
- spring onions (scallions)

Method

1. Combine the rice, cooked rice, coconut, salt and hot water in a bowl. Set aside to cool. Grind the mixture to a fine consistency.
2. Grease an *idli* mould. Heat the mould in a steamer for 5 minutes. Pour in the rice mixture, cover and steam for 5 minutes until firm. Repeat with remaining rice mixture.
3. Remove the cake from the mould and set aside.
4. To serve, top each rice cake with Prawn (Shrimp) Topping and a teaspoon of Coconut Milk Topping.
5. Garnish with red chillies, coriander leaves, pumpkin and spring onions (scallions).

Chef's note: Shallow round muffin tins can be used if *idli* mould is not available.

*Prawn (Shrimp) Topping

- 250 grams | 9 ounces small prawns (shrimps), shelled, deveined and chopped
- 100 grams | 3½ ounces | 1 cup grated, peeled coconut
- 2 tablespoons cooking oil
- 1 tablespoon finely ground, peeled garlic
- 1 tablespoon chopped coriander roots, finely ground
- 1 teaspoon white peppercorns, finely ground
- 3 kaffir lime leaves, finely sliced
- 1 tablespoon crushed palm sugar (jaggery) or brown sugar
- 1 teaspoon salt

Method

1. Mix the prawns (shrimps) with the coconut.
2. Heat the cooking oil, fry the garlic, coriander roots and pepper until fragrant.
3. Add the prawns (shrimps) and coconut mixture, kaffir lime leaves, palm sugar (jaggery) or brown sugar and salt. Mix well.

**Coconut Milk Topping

- 1 portion thick coconut milk (refer to page 78)
- 85 grams | 3 ounces | ⅓ cup sugar
- ½ teaspoon salt

Method

Mix all the ingredients to a smooth consistency.

(Clockwise from top) Khanom Krok (Steamed Rice Cake with Savoury Toppings), Kang Rau Punk (Yam Puffs), chilli sauce.

Kao Man Som Tam Malakor
(Unripe Papaya Salad)

Salad Dish | 15-minute Preparation | Serves 4

Ingredients

500 grams | 1 pound, 1 1/2 ounces unripe papaya, peeled and finely shredded

1 tablespoon tamarind juice, extracted from 1 teaspoon tamarind pulp and 1 tablespoon water

3 tablespoons crushed palm sugar (jaggery) or brown sugar

2 tablespoons lemon juice

3 tablespoons fish sauce (nam pla)

80 grams | 2 3/4 ounces | 1/2 cup dried prawns (shrimps), soaked in hot water, drained and coarsely pounded

5 kalamansi, cut into small cubes

100 grams | 3 1/2 ounces cabbage, sliced

100 grams | 3 1/2 ounces long beans, cut into 5-cm | 2-inch lengths

100 grams | 3 1/2 ounces lettuce, torn into pieces

100 grams | 3 1/2 ounces sweet basil leaves (bai horapa)

5–6 cherry tomatoes

Coarsely Pounded Paste

2 small tomatoes, quartered

6 cloves garlic, peeled

4 bird's eye chillies

6 white peppercorns

85 grams | 3 ounces | 1/2 cup roasted peanuts

Method

1. Gently crush the papaya in a mortar with a pestle and set aside.
2. Combine the tamarind juice, palm sugar (jaggery) or brown sugar, lemon juice and fish sauce. Add the coarsely pounded paste and mix well.
3. Add the crushed papaya, dried prawns (shrimps) and kalamansi cubes and toss well.
4. Serve with a mixture of cabbage, long beans, lettuce, sweet basil leaves and cherry tomatoes.

Prawn (Shrimp) and Sponge Gourd (Loofah) Curry

Main Dish | 20-minute Preparation | 15-minute Cooking | Serves 4

Ingredients

400 grams | 14 ounces | 4 cups grated, peeled coconut

375 ml | 12 fl oz | 1 1/2 cups water

125 ml | 4 fl oz | 1/2 cup cooking oil

2 tablespoons fish sauce (nam pla)

1 1/2 tablespoons crushed palm sugar (jaggery) or brown sugar

2 kaffir lime leaves

2 tomatoes, quartered

300 grams | 10 1/2 ounces medium tiger prawns (shrimps), feelers and legs removed

210 grams | 7 1/2 ounces peeled, cubed sponge gourd (loofah)

2 red chillies, halved lengthways

1 sprig sweet basil leaves (bai horapa)

Finely Ground Paste

8 dried chillies, seeded, soaked in hot water and drained

1 teaspoon salt

1.5 cm | 3/4 inch galangal, peeled

1 stalk lemon grass, chopped

1.5 cm | 3/4 inch dried shrimp paste

Method

1. Add 125 ml / 4 fl oz / 1/2 cup water to the grated coconut to extract thick coconut milk. Set aside.
2. Add the remaining water to the grated coconut to extract thin coconut milk.
3. Heat the cooking oil, fry the finely ground paste until fragrant and the oil floats on top.
4. Add the fish sauce, palm sugar (jaggery) or brown sugar, kaffir lime leaves, tomatoes, prawns (shrimps) and thin coconut milk and cook for 10 minutes.
5. Add the sponge gourd (loofah) and red chillies and mix well. Add the thick coconut milk and cook over a low heat for 5 minutes.
6. Remove from heat, add the sweet basil leaves and stir well.
7. Serve with rice.

Chef's note: Fish or squid may be substituted for the prawns (shrimps).

(Clockwise from top right) Kao Man Som Tam Malakor (Unripe Papaya Salad), Prawn (Shrimp) and Sponge Gourd (Loofah) Curry, vegetable platter.

Rice Vermicelli in Coconut Milk

Noodle Dish | 20-minute Preparation |
20-minute Cooking | Serves 4

Ingredients

55 grams | 2 ounces tamarind pulp

2 tablespoons water

1 portion boiled coconut cream
(refer to page 78)

6 shallots, peeled and chopped

100 grams | 3^1/2 ounces chicken fillet,
thinly sliced

150 grams | 5^1/2 ounces medium tiger
prawns (shrimps), shelled and
deveined

2 tablespoons preserved soy bean paste
(*tau jiew nam*)

2 tablespoons sugar

2 tablespoons powdered chilli

250 grams | 9 ounces rice vermicelli,
soaked in water for 15 minutes or
until soft, then drained

2 pieces bean curd, fried in 90 ml |
3 fl oz | 3/8 cup cooking oil, then
finely diced

100 grams | 3^1/2 ounces Chinese chives,
cut into 2.5-cm | 1-inch lengths

50 grams | 1^2/3 ounces coriander leaves
(cilantro), cut into 1-cm | 1/2-inch
lengths

2 eggs, beaten, fried into thin omelettes
and cut into strips

300 grams | 10^1/2 ounces bean sprouts,
tailed

2 lemons, cut in wedges

1 banana blossom (*dok kluai*), tough
outer layers discarded, shredded
then blanched and drained

Method

1. Combine the tamarind pulp and
water and extract the juice. Set
aside.
2. Heat the boiled coconut cream for 5
minutes, add the shallots and stir-fry
until fragrant. Add the chicken and
the prawns (shrimps) and continue
stir-frying for 2 minutes.

3. Add the preserved soy bean paste,
sugar, powdered chilli and tamarind
juice and mix well into a sauce.
Divide sauce into 2 portions and
keep one portion aside.
4. Add rice vermicelli, bean curd and
Chinese chives to one portion of the
sauce and cook for 1 minute.
5. Transfer to a serving dish and pour
the reserved sauce on top of the
vermicelli.
6. Garnish with coriander leaves
(cilantro) and omelette strips.
7. Serve with bean sprouts, lemon
wedges and blanched banana
blossom.

Chaw Muang
(Steamed Blue Rose Tea Cake)

Side Dish | 25-minute Preparation |
20-minute Cooking | Serves 4

Ingredients

10 butterfly / blue pea flowers (*anjan*)

125 ml | 4 fl oz | 1/2 cup hot water

1 tablespoon lime juice

240 grams | 8^1/2 ounces | 2 cups
rice flour, sifted

1 tablespoon tapioca flour, sifted

1 tablespoon arrowroot flour, sifted

250 ml | 8 fl oz | 1 cup water

Chicken and Prawn (Shrimp) Filling*

banana leaves

parsley

carrot, carved into flower shape

red chilli, carved into flower shape

Method

1. Soak the butterfly / blue pea flowers
in hot water for 10 minutes. Strain
to get the blue colouring. Add the
lime juice and mix well.
2. Combine the rice flour, tapioca flour
and arrowroot flour. Add blue
colouring and water to form a thin
paste.
3. Cook the paste over a medium heat
and stir constantly until it thickens
and becomes a slightly elastic dough.
Remove from heat and set aside to
cool.

4. Divide the dough into small balls,
about 3.5 cm / 1^1/2 inches in
diameter each. Cover with a damp
cloth.
5. Flatten a ball of dough into a thin
sheet and place 1 teaspoon of
Chicken and Prawn (Shrimp) Filling
on top. Wrap the sheet around the
filling and roll into a ball. Pinch with
a pastry pincer and shape to
resemble a rose.
6. Arrange the tea cakes on a steamer
lined with banana leaves. Sprinkle
with cold water and steam over
rapidly boiling water for about 8
minutes.
7. Garnish with parsley, carrot and red
chilli before serving.

*Chicken and Prawn (Shrimp) Filling

60 ml | 2 fl oz | 1/4 cup cooking oil

1 large onion, peeled and finely chopped

2 cloves garlic, peeled and finely
chopped

1 coriander root, finely chopped

200 grams | 7 ounces minced (ground)
chicken

200 grams | 7 ounces minced (ground),
shelled prawns (shrimps)

1 teaspoon ground white pepper

3 tablespoons sugar

5 tablespoons fish sauce (*nam pla*)

70 grams | 2^1/2 ounces | 1/2 cup ground,
roasted peanuts

Method

1. Heat the cooking oil and sauté the
onion, garlic and coriander root until
fragrant.
2. Add the chicken and prawns
(shrimps), pepper, sugar, fish sauce
and peanuts, stir-fry until dry. Set
aside to cool.

Chef's note: Tea cakes may be served with boiled
coconut cream (refer to page 78).

(Clockwise from top right) Vegetables—banana blossom, lemon and coriander leaves, Rice Vermicelli in Coconut Milk, Chaw Muang (Steamed Blue Rose Tea Cake).

Yam Nua
(Sweet and Sour Barbecued Beef Salad)

Salad Dish | 30-minute Preparation |
20-minute Cooking | Serves 4

Ingredients

500 grams | 1 pound, 1¹/₂ ounces round
  rump or sirloin beef steak, grilled
  (broiled) and finely sliced

2 large white onions, peeled, halved and
  finely sliced

50 grams | 2 ounces coriander leaves
  (cilantro), cut into 1-cm | ¹/₂-inch
  lengths

1 red chilli, seeded, cut into 5-cm |
  2-inch strips and soaked in cold
  water

4 lettuce leaves

2 cucumbers, peeled and sliced

Salad Dressing (combined)

10 cloves garlic, peeled and coarsely
  chopped

20 bird's eye chillies, coarsely chopped

3 tablespoons fish sauce (*nam pla*)

3 tablespoons lemon or lime juice

2 tablespoons sugar

Method

1. Pour salad dressing over the beef
   slices and mix well. Add the onions,
   coriander leaves (cilantro) and chilli
   strips and toss well.
2. Transfer salad onto a lettuce lined
   plate. Arrange cucumber on the
   sides. Serve chilled.

Chef's note: Seasonings for the salad dressing
may be adjusted to suit your taste.
    The salad dressing may be served separately
in a bowl.

Pineapple Rice

Rice Dish | 15-minute Preparation |
30-minute Cooking | Serves 4

Ingredients

375 grams | 13 ounces | 1¹/₂ cups
  fragrant Thai rice, washed and
  drained

625 ml | 20 fl oz | 2¹/₂ cups water

1 (1.5 kilogram | 3 pounds, 4¹/₂ ounces)
  medium ripe pineapple

3 tablespoons cooking oil

10 shallots, peeled and sliced

85 grams | 3 ounces | ¹/₂ cup dried
  prawns (shrimps), soaked in hot
  water for 5 minutes, drained and
  chopped

280 grams | 10 ounces chicken breast,
  cut into small cubes

4 chicken sausages, cut into small cubes

3 tablespoons fish sauce (*nam pla*)

2 tablespoons meat curry powder
  (optional)

60 ml | 2 fl oz | ¹/₄ cup light soy sauce

¹/₂ teaspoon monosodium glutamate

1¹/₂ tablespoons sugar

lettuce

carrot, carved into flower shape

55 grams | 2 ounces coriander leaves
  (cilantro), chopped

1 red chilli, cut into small strips and
  soaked in cold water

Method

1. Combine the rice and water and
   cook. Fluff the rice and set aside to
   cool.
2. Cut the pineapple in half lengthways.
   Run a knife around the edge of the
   pineapple, cut and scoop out the
   flesh. Cut the flesh into 1-cm /
   ¹/₂-inch cubes to fill 1 cup. Keep the
   shell (casing) aside.
3. Heat the cooking oil and fry shallots
   until brown and crisp. Set aside. In
   the same oil sauté the dried prawns
   until fragrant. Add the chicken and
   sausage cubes and fry until the
   chicken is cooked.
4. Add the fish sauce, meat curry
   powder (optional), soy sauce,
   monosodium glutamate, sugar and
   cooked rice. Mix well. Add pineapple
   cubes and continue frying for 2–3
   minutes. Set aside.
5. Heat the pineapple shell (casing) in a
   180°C / 350°F preheated oven for 10
   minutes. Remove from the oven and
   fill with the pineapple fried rice.
6. Garnish the rice with lettuce, carrot ,
   crisp-fried shallots, coriander leaves
   (cilantro) and chilli strips.

(Anticlockwise from top) Pineapple Rice, Yam Nua (Sweet and Sour Barbecued Beef Salad), cucumber slices.

Claypot Crabs with Glass Noodles

Main Dish | 20-minute Preparation |
20-minute Cooking | Serves 4

Ingredients

- 500 grams | 1 pound, 1½ ounces crabs, cleaned
- 3 tablespoons cooking oil
- 55 grams | 2 ounces glass noodles (*woon sen*), soaked in water for 5 minutes and drained
- 375 ml | 12 fl oz | 1½ cups chicken stock (refer to page 78)
- 1 sprig coriander leaves (cilantro), cut into 1-cm | ½-inch lengths
- 1 red chilli, seeded and cut into thin strips

Seasoning (blended)

- 2 tablespoons fish sauce (*nam pla*)
- 2 tablespoons sesame oil
- ½ teaspoon monosodium glutamate
- 1 tablespoon Lea & Perrins sauce
- 1 tablespoon light soy sauce

Finely Ground Paste

- 1 tablespoon black peppercorns
- 1 cm | ½ inch ginger, peeled
- 3 coriander roots, chopped
- 3 cloves garlic, peeled

Method

1. Marinate the crabs with the seasoning for 30 minutes.
2. Heat the cooking oil in a clay pot and fry the finely ground paste for 5 minutes or until fragrant.
3. Add the marinated crabs, glass noodles and chicken stock. Stir well.
4. Cover the pot and simmer for 8 minutes. Garnish with coriander leaves (cilantro) and chilli strips. Serve hot.

Chef's note: Chicken may be substituted for the crabs.

Sah Khoo Sai Mooh
(Steamed Sago Balls with Meat Filling)

Side Dish | 75-minute Preparation |
35-minute Cooking | Serves 6

Ingredients

- 200 grams | 7 ounces | 1 cup pearl sago, washed in cold water and drained
- 200 ml | 7 fl oz | ⅘ cup hot water
- Meat Filling*
- banana leaves, cut into small squares
- 3 tablespoons vegetable oil
- 3 cloves garlic, peeled, fried in 60 ml | 2 fl oz | ¼ cup cooking oil and drained
- 2 red chillies, seeded and chopped
- 5 bird's eye chillies
- pumpkin, carved into flower shaper
- papaya, carved into leaf shape

Method

1. Place the pearl sago in a bowl and add hot (not boiling) water, a little at a time, stirring constantly and soak for about 5 minutes. Knead into a dough and set aside for 1 hour.
2. Roll the dough into small balls about 1 cm / ½ inch in diameter each. Set aside.
3. Flatten a sago ball into a thin sheet and place 1 heaped teaspoon of Meat Filling on top. Wrap the sago sheet around the filling and roll into a ball. Place each ball onto a piece of banana leaf square brushed with vegetable oil. Repeat until all the ingredients are used up.
4. Steam over rapidly boiling water for about 15 minutes.
5. Remove the balls from the steamer and sprinkle with fried garlic and chopped chillies.
6. Serve on a dish and garnish with bird's eye chillies, pumpkin and papaya.

*Meat Filling

- 3 tablespoons cooking oil
- 1 teaspoon chopped coriander root
- 10 cloves garlic, peeled and finely sliced
- 100 grams | 3½ ounces minced (ground) beef or chicken
- 3 tablespoons crushed palm sugar (jaggery) or brown sugar
- 3 tablespoons fish sauce (*nam pla*)
- 200 grams | 7 ounces shallots, peeled and finely chopped
- ¼ teaspoon ground white pepper
- 55 grams | 2 ounces | ⅓ cup roasted peanuts, coarsely pounded

Method

1. Heat the cooking oil and sauté the coriander root and garlic until fragrant or light brown.
2. Add the beef or chicken, palm sugar (jaggery) or brown sugar, fish sauce, shallots and white pepper and stir-fry until dry. Add the peanuts and mix well.

Chef's note: Instead of steaming, the sago balls can be cooked directly in hot boiling water. Sago balls will float to the top once they are cooked. Drain thoroughly. Sprinkle with the fried garlic and chopped chillies before serving.

(From top) Claypot Crabs with Glass Noodles, Sah Khoo Sai Mooh (Steamed Sago Balls with Meat Filling).

Ba Mee Nong Kai
(Chicken Drumstick and Noodle Soup)

Soup Dish | 45-minute Preparation |
30-minute Cooking | Serves 6

Ingredients

- 1 kilogram | 2 pounds, 3 ounces chicken drumsticks
- 2 tablespoon light soy sauce
- 3 tablespoons dark soy sauce
- 2 tablespoon seasoning sauce
- 2 tablespoons whiskey (optional)
- 2 teaspoons ground black pepper
- 3 teaspoons salt
- 2 tablespoons sugar
- 2.5 litres | 80 fl oz | 10 cups water
- 200 grams | 7 ounces mustard green, cut into 7.5-cm | 3-inch lengths
- 300 grams | 10½ ounces | 2 cups plain (all-purpose) flour, sifted
- 1 litre | 32 fl oz | 4 cups cooking oil
- 2 egg yolks
- red chilli, seeded and chopped

Method

1. Season the chicken drumsticks with 1 tablespoon light soy sauce, 2 tablespoons dark soy sauce, 1 tablespoon seasoning sauce, whiskey (optional), pepper, 1 teaspoon salt and sugar and marinate for about 1 hour.
2. Bring 85 ml / 2½ fl oz / ⅓ cup water to a boil and blanch the mustard leaves. Drain the leaves and reserve the boiling water.
3. Combine the flour, 1 teaspoon salt, 1 tablespoon cooking oil, egg yolks and reserved boiling water and knead the mixture to form a dough. Roll the dough through a noodle maker to make thin noodles, sprinkle with flour to keep from sticking together.
4. Bring 1.5 litres / 48 fl oz / 6 cups water to a boil. Add the remaining salt before adding the noodles.
5. Drain the noodles, add 2 tablespoons cooking oil and toss to keep from sticking together. Set the noodles aside.
6. Heat the remaining cooking oil and fry the marinated chicken until brown. Drain and set aside.
7. Add the remaining water to the marinade and bring to a boil. Stir in the remaining light and dark soy sauce and seasoning sauce before adding the chicken. Simmer for about 15 minutes over low heat.
8. To serve, place some noodles in a soup bowl, top with mustard leaves, a chicken drumstick and hot soup. Sprinkle with chopped red chilli.

Chef's note: Ready-to-use spinach noodles are available from vegetarian grocers.

Mutton (Lamb) Tripe Curry

Main Dish | 20-minute Preparation |
45-minute Cooking | Serves 6

Ingredients

- 500 grams | 1 pound, 1½ ounces mutton (lamb) tripe, cut into 2.5-cm | 1-inch pieces
- 2 tablespoons slaked lime, mixed with 1.25 litres | 40 fl oz | 5 cups water
- 10 lemon grass leaves
- 10 fresh bay leaves
- 1.5 litres | 48 fl oz | 6 cups water
- 45 grams | 1½ ounces | ⅓ cup tapioca flour, blended with 2 tablespoons water
- 5 kaffir lime leaves + extra for garnishing
- 2 red chillies, finely sliced
- 1 tablespoon salt
- 6 stalks lemon grass, finely sliced
- 1 red chilli, carved into flower shape

Finely Ground Paste

- 20 cloves garlic, smoked and peeled
- 10 shallots, peeled
- 2 coriander roots, chopped
- 20 white peppercorns
- 6 red chillies
- 2 tablespoons crushed palm sugar (jaggery) or brown sugar
- 2 tablespoons fish sauce (*nam pla*)
- 1.5 sq cm | ¾ sq inch dried shrimp paste
- 1.5 cm | ¾ inch galangal, peeled
- 125 grams | 4½ ounces steamed salted Indian mackerel fish or any preserved fish, de-boned and shredded

Method

1. Soak the mutton (lamb) tripe in the lime water for 20 minutes. Wash thoroughly. Cook for 30 minutes in a pressure cooker with 1 litre / 32 fl oz / 4 cups water. Drain.
2. Pound the lemon grass leaves and bay leaves together. Add 60 ml / 2 fl oz / ¼ cup water, squeeze and extract the juice.
3. Mix the juice with the finely ground paste, add the remaining water and bring to a boil.
4. Add the cooked tripe and boil for 5 minutes.
5. Stir in the tapioca mixture to thicken the sauce. Add the kaffir lime leaves, red chilli slices and salt. Cook for 5 minutes.
6. Garnish with lemon grass slices, red chilli and kaffir lime leaves

Chef's note: If you prefer to cook the tripe in a pot instead of a pressure cooker increase cooking time by an hour and increase water by an additional 1 litre / 32 fl oz / 4 cups.

(From top) Ba Mee Nong Kai (Chicken Drumstick and Noodle Soup), Mutton (Lamb) Tripe Curry.

Asparagus in Coconut Cream and Lemon Grass Sauce

Vegetable Dish | 15-minute Preparation | 20-minute Cooking | Serves 4

Ingredients

180 ml | 6 fl oz | 3/4 cup water

125 grams | 4 1/2 ounces | 1 1/4 cups grated, peeled coconut

2 tablespoons cooking oil

2 stalks lemon grass, finely sliced

2 cloves garlic, peeled and finely sliced

1.5 cm | 3/4 inch young ginger, peeled and finely sliced

150 grams | 5 1/2 ounces prawns (shrimps), shelled and deveined

500 grams | 1 pound, 1 1/2 ounces asparagus spears, cut into 5-cm | 2-inch lengths

250 grams | 9 ounces bean sprouts, tailed, blanched and drained

1 red chilli, finely sliced

Method

1. Combine the water and grated coconut and extract 250 ml / 8 fl oz / 1 cup coconut milk.
2. Heat the cooking oil, fry the lemon grass, garlic and ginger until fragrant.
3. Add the asparagus, prawns (shrimps) and coconut milk and bring to a boil. Simmer on medium heat for 5 minutes or until the asparagus is tender.
4. Arrange the blanched bean sprouts on a serving plate, top with asparagus and garnish with red chilli slices.

Kai Song Kreung
(Thai Stuffed Eggs)

Side Dish | 20-minute Preparation | 20-minute Cooking | Serves 6

Ingredients

6 hard-boiled eggs

60 grams | 2 ounces minced (ground) chicken

60 grams | 2 ounces minced (ground), shelled prawns (shrimps)

1 tablespoon minced (ground), peeled garlic

1 teaspoon ground white pepper

2 tablespoons fish sauce (*nam pla*)

2 tablespoons cornflour (cornstarch)

1 teaspoon sugar

1 tablespoon finely chopped coriander roots

2 sprigs coriander leaves (cilantro)

1 red chilli, cut into rings

435 ml | 14 fl oz | 1 3/4 cups cooking oil

10 lettuce leaves

2 tomatoes, sliced into rings

Method

1. Halve the eggs lengthways with shell still intact. Scoop out the yolks and keep aside the egg white casings.
2. Mix the egg yolks, chicken, prawns (shrimps), garlic, pepper, fish sauce, cornflour (cornstarch), sugar and coriander roots into a smooth paste.
3. Stuff egg white casings with the paste and spread evenly. Repeat until all the ingredients are used up.
4. Fry the stuffed eggs over medium heat for about 8 minutes or until slightly brown. Drain and cool, remove shells. Garnish with red chilli and coriander leaves (cilantro).
5. Serve on a bed of lettuce leaves and tomatoes.

(From top) Kai Song Kreung (Thai Stuffed Eggs), Asparagus in Coconut Cream and Lemon Grass Sauce.

Pla Lard Prik
(Fried Fish a' la Thai)

Main Dish | 20-minute Preparation |
20-minute Cooking | Serves 4

Ingredients

1 (700 grams | 1½ pounds) black pomfret or garoupa, cleaned and gutted

60 ml | 2 fl oz | ¼ cup fish sauce (*nam pla*)

½ tablespoon ground white pepper

1 egg white, lightly beaten

110 grams | 4 ounces | ¾ cup cornflour (cornstarch)

375 ml | 12 fl oz | 1½ cups cooking oil

55 grams | 2 ounces tamarind pulp

85 ml | 2½ fl oz | ⅓ cup water

1 stalk lemon grass, bruised

2 tablespoons crushed palm sugar (jaggery) or brown sugar

2½ tablespoons sugar

salt

10 lettuce leaves

55 grams | 2 ounces coriander leaves (cilantro)

1 red chilli, seeded, cut into thin strips and soaked in cold water

Finely Ground Paste

9 red chillies

4 bird's eye chillies

½ teaspoon salt

2.5 cm | 1 inch galangal, peeled

2 coriander roots

9 white peppercorns

4 cloves garlic, peeled

6 shallots, peeled

Method

1. Slit both sides of the fish and marinate with 1 tablespoon fish sauce and pepper for 30 minutes.
2. Dip in beaten egg white and coat with cornflour (cornstarch). Deep-fry until crisp and golden brown. Drain well. Reserve the oil.
3. Combine the tamarind pulp and water and extract the juice. Set aside.
4. Heat 125 ml / 4 fl oz / ½ cup of the reserved oil and fry the finely ground paste and lemon grass until fragrant and the oil floats on top. Season with the remaining fish sauce, palm sugar (jaggery) or brown sugar, salt and tamarind juice. Cook over low heat for 5 minutes.
5. Place fish on a lettuce lined plate, pour sauce on fish. Garnish with coriander leaves (cilantro) and red chilli strips.

Beef Curry with Pineapple and Eggplant

Main Dish | 20-minute Preparation |
15-minute Cooking | Serves 6

Ingredients

1 portion boiled coconut cream (refer to page 78)

1 portion red curry paste (*Nam Prik Gaeng Ped*, page 78)

500 grams | 1 pound, 1½ ounces beef tenderloin, cut into 1.5 cm / ¾ inch thick slices

1 portion thin coconut milk (refer to page 78)

1 medium long eggplant, halved lengthways, then cut into 2.5-cm | 1-inch lengths

4 bird's eye chillies + 5–6 extra for garnishing

3 red chillies, sliced into rounds

300 grams | 10½ ounces peeled pineapple, cut into 2.5-cm | 1-inch cubes

1 sprig sweet basil leaves (*bai horapa*)

red chilli strips

Method

1. Heat the boiled coconut cream for 5 minutes and fry the red curry paste until fragrant.
2. Add the beef, thin coconut milk, eggplant and bird's eye chillies, cook until beef is tender.
3. Add the red chillies and pineapple cubes, cook for 5 minutes.
4. Garnish with bird's eye chillies, sweet basil leaves and chilli strips.

(From top) Pla Lard Prik (Fried Fish a'la Thai), Beef Curry with Pineapple and Eggplant.

Mee Krob
(Crispy Fried Vermicelli)

Noodle Dish | 25-minute Preparation |
15-minute Cooking | Serves 4

Ingredients

810 ml | 26 fl oz | 3¼ cups cooking oil

200 grams | 7 ounces rice vermicelli

3 cloves pickled garlic, finely chopped

3 shallots, peeled and finely chopped

100 grams | 3½ ounces chicken fillet, finely diced

150 grams | 5½ ounces prawns (shrimps), shelled and deveined

1 tablespoon preserved soy bean (*tau jiew*), mashed

1 tablespoon vinegar

2 tablespoons fish sauce (*nam pla*)

80 grams | 2¾ ounces | ⅓ cup crushed palm sugar (jaggery) or brown sugar

1 tablespoon powdered chilli

1 tablespoon lemon or lime juice

1 piece bean curd, cut into thin strips and deep-fried until crisp

100 grams | 3½ ounces coriander leaves (cilantro), cut into 1-cm | ½-inch lengths

50 grams | 2 ounces Chinese chives, cut into 2.5-cm | 1-inch lengths

150 grams | 5½ ounces bean sprouts, tailed

1 cucumber, sliced

Method

1. Heat 750 ml | 24 fl oz | 3 cups cooking oil, deep-fry the rice vermicelli, a handful at a time, until crisp. Drain well and set aside.
2. Heat the remaining cooking oil, sauté the chopped pickled garlic and shallots until fragrant and slightly brown.
3. Add the chicken and prawns (shrimps) and stir-fry for about 2 minutes. Stir in the preserved soy bean, vinegar, fish sauce, palm sugar (jaggery) or brown sugar and powdered chilli. Add the lemon or lime juice.
4. Reduce the heat and add the deep-fried vermicelli and fried bean curd and mix well.
5. Garnish with Chinese chives, bean sprouts and cucumber.

Chef's note: You can also garnish this noodle with coriander leaves, pickled garlic slices and red chilli strips.

Kaeng Liang
(Thai Vegetable Soup)

Soup Dish | 15-minute Preparation |
25-minute Cooking | Serves 6

Ingredients

1.25 litres | 40 fl oz | 5 cups chicken stock (refer to page 78) or water

1 stalk lemon grass, bruised

60 ml | 2 fl oz | ¼ cup fish sauce (*nam pla*)

1 carrot, peeled and cut into 3.5-cm | 1½-inch lengths

4 bird's eye chillies

500 grams | 1 pound, 1½ ounces bottle gourd (sponge gourd), peeled and cut into 5-cm | 2-inch strips

150 grams | 5½ ounces fresh oyster mushrooms

8 baby corn cobs, cut into 3.5-cm | 1½-inch lengths

2 sprigs sweet basil leaves (*bai horapa*)

salt

crisp-fried shallots

bird's eye chillies

red chilli, chopped

Finely Ground Paste

10 white peppercorns

2.5 sq cm | 1 sq inch dried shrimp paste

3 tablespoons fish sauce (*nam pla*)

10 shallots, peeled

150 grams | 5½ ounces | 1 cup dried prawns (shrimps), soaked in water and drained

Method

1. Bring the chicken stock or water to a boil, add the finely ground paste and lemon grass and simmer for 15 minutes.
2. Add fish sauce, carrot and bird's eye chillies and boil for 3 minutes.
3. Add the bottle gourd (sponge gourd), mushrooms and baby corn and boil for 5 minutes.
4. Stir in the sweet basil leaves. Season with salt.
5. Serve hot, garnished with crisp-fried shallots, bird's eye chillies and chopped red chilli.

(Anticlockwise from top right) Kaeng Liang (Thai Vegetable Soup) in individual bowl and serving bowl, Mee Krob (Crispy Fried Vermicelli).

Tom Yam Pla Thoy Poh
(Thai Fish Chowder)

Soup Dish | 15-minute Preparation | 25-minute Cooking | Serves 6

Ingredients

2 tablespoons cooking oil

15 dried chillies

6 cloves garlic, peeled

8 shallots, peeled

1 litre | 32 fl oz | 4 cups chicken stock (refer to page 78)

3 coriander roots, bruised

3 stalks lemon grass, bruised and halved

5 kaffir lime leaves

5 cm | 2 inches galangal, peeled and finely sliced

60 ml | 2 fl oz | 1/4 cup fish sauce (*nam pla*)

8 bird's eye chillies, bruised

1 teaspoon salt

500 grams | 1 pound, 1 1/2 ounces Spanish mackerel fillet, cut into 2.5-cm | 1-inch pieces

100 grams | 3 1/2 ounces coriander leaves (cilantro), cut into 1-cm | 1/2-inch lengths

Method

1. Heat the cooking oil and stir-fry dried chillies until crisp. Remove and drain well.
2. In the same oil, fry the garlic and shallots for about 2–3 minutes or until light brown. Remove and drain well.
3. Combine the fried dried chillies, garlic and shallots and grind together to a fine paste.
4. Bring the chicken stock to a boil. Add the coriander roots, lemon grass, kaffir lime leaves, galangal, fish sauce, bird's eye chillies and salt. Stir well and continue to boil for about 5 minutes.
5. Add ground paste and mackerel and cook for another 5 minutes.
6. Garnish with coriander leaves (cilantro) and serve.

How Mok Pla
(Thai Fish Paste in Banana Leaf Casing)

Side Dish | 20-minute Preparation | 10-minute Cooking | Serves 6

Ingredients

400 grams | 14 ounces | 4 cups grated, peeled coconut

300 ml | 10 fl oz | 1 1/4 cups water

1 teaspoon rice flour

500 grams | 1 pound, 1 1/2 ounces minced (ground) Spanish mackerel or red snapper

140 grams | 5 ounces red curry paste (*Nam Prik Gaeng Ped*, page 78)

1 tablespoon chopped coriander roots

3 kaffir lime leaves, thinly sliced + extra for garnishing

6 lesser ginger (*kra chai*), peeled and finely chopped (optional)

2 small (70 grams | 2 1/2 ounces) eggs, beaten

60 ml | 2 fl oz | 1/4 cup fish sauce (*nam pla*)

banana leaves, cut into 9-cm | 3 1/2-inch rounds and made into casings

200 grams | 7 ounces cabbage leaves, shredded and blanched

100 grams | 3 1/2 ounces pointed pepper leaves (*cha plu*)

55 grams | 2 ounces coriander leaves (cilantro)

1 red chilli, cut in round slices

water melon, carved into flower shape

radish, carved into leaf shape

Method

1. Combine the coconut and water and extract 400 ml | 13 fl oz | 1 3/5 cups coconut milk.
2. Add rice flour to 100 ml | 3 1/2 fl oz / 2/5 cup of the coconut milk and cook over low heat for 1 minute. Set aside to cool.
3. In an earthen or ceramic pot, mix the fish with red curry paste, coriander roots, kaffir lime leaves, lesser ginger (optional) and beaten egg. Add the remaining coconut milk, a little bit at a time. Add fish sauce. Mix well for 5–10 minutes until the paste becomes sticky.
4. To assemble, fill a banana casing with shredded cabbage, a pointed pepper leaf and some fish paste and steam for 5 minutes. Top with the cooked coconut milk and rice flour mixture and add coriander leaves (cilantro), red chillies and kaffir lime leaves slices.
5. Steam again for 5 minutes.
6. Serve garnished with water melon and radish.

(From top) Tom Yam Pla Thoy Poh (Thai Fish Chowder), How Mok Pla (Thai Fish Paste in Banana Leaf Casing).

Yum Kob Tam
(Spicy Chicken Salad)

Salad Dish | 20-minute Preparation |
10-minute Cooking | Serves 4

Ingredients

- 110 grams | 4 ounces | 1 cup grated, peeled coconut
- 60 ml | 2 fl oz | 1/4 cup water
- 10 bird's eye chillies, coarsely pounded
- 2 tablespoons all-purpose roasted chilli paste (Nam Prik Pau, page 78)
- 2 tablespoons fish sauce (nam pla)
- 1 tablespoon crushed palm sugar (jaggery) or brown sugar
- 3 tablespoons lemon or lime juice
- 250 grams | 9 ounces chicken breast, boiled for 10 minutes or until tender, then finely shredded
- 6 stalks lemon grass, finely sliced
- 4 kaffir lime leaves, finely sliced
- 50 grams | 2 ounces coriander leaves (cilantro), finely sliced
- 100 grams | 3 1/2 ounces mint leaves, finely sliced + extra for garnishing
- 10 lettuce leaves
- 2 tomatoes, wedged
- 3 red chillies, seeded, cut into strips
- 1 cucumber, carved into leaf shape
- radish, carved into flower shape

Method

1. Combine the coconut and water to extract 60 ml / 2 fl oz / 1/4 cup coconut milk.
2. Blend the bird's eye chillies, all-purpose roasted chilli paste, fish sauce, palm sugar (jaggery) or brown sugar, lemon or lime juice and coconut milk into a salty-sour dressing.
3. Mix the chicken with lemon grass, kaffir lime leaves, coriander leaves (cilantro) and mint.
4. Add the dressing and mix well. Serve on a dish lined with lettuce leaves.
5. Garnish with tomatoes, red chilli stripes, mint, cucumber and radish.

Chef's note: This salad may be served as a starter (appetiser).

Ngob Tha Lae
(Baked Seafood Wrapped in Banana Leaf)

Main Dish | 15-minute Preparation |
15-minute Cooking | Serves 6

Ingredients

- banana leaf
- aluminium foil
- 5 kaffir lime leaves, finely sliced
- 2 red chillies, cut into fine strips
- Seafood Filling*
- 100 grams | 3 1/2 ounces shelled sea mussels, boiled
- 250 grams | 9 ounces cabbage, shredded and blanched
- 2 sprigs sweet basil leaves (bai horapa), stalks removed
- 1 spring onion (scallions)
- carrot, carved into flower shape
- lemon, wedged
- lettuce, sliced

Method

1. Cut the banana leaf and aluminium foil into 15 x 20-cm / 6 x 8-inch rectangles. Place the banana leaf on top of the aluminium foil.
2. Layer sliced kaffir lime leaves and red chilli strips in the middle of the banana leaf, add 3 tablespoons of Seafood Filling, 3 sea mussels, cabbage and sweet basil leaves. Top with 1 tablespoon of Seafood Filling. Form into a square.
3. Bake or grill (broil) for 20 minutes.
4. To serve, cut open the foil to resemble a flower. Sprinkle with lettuces slices and garnish with spring onion (scallion), carrot and lemon.

*Seafood Filling

- 1 portion boiled coconut cream (refer page 78)
- 100 grams | 3 1/2 ounces small prawns (shrimps), shelled and deveined
- 100 grams | 3 1/2 ounces crabmeat, shredded
- 100 grams | 3 1/2 ounces fish fillet, cut into 2.5-cm | 1-inch pieces
- 2 tablespoons fish sauce (nam pla)
- 1 tablespoon crushed palm sugar (jaggery) or brown sugar
- 2 eggs, beaten

Finely Ground Paste

- 10 red chillies, seeded
- 3.5 cm | 1 1/2 inches galangal, peeled
- 3 stalks lemon grass, sliced
- 6 shallots, peeled
- 15 cloves garlic, peeled
- 1 coriander root, chopped
- 1 cm | 1/2 inch dried shrimp paste
- 1 teaspoon chopped, peeled lesser ginger (kra chai)

Method

1. Heat the boiled coconut cream for 5 minutes. Add the finely ground paste and stir-fry until fragrant.
2. Add the prawns (shrimps), crabmeat, fish, fish sauce, palm sugar (jaggery) or brown sugar.
3. Remove from heat and add in the beaten egg. Mix well and set aside.

(From top) Ngob Tha Lae (Baked Seafood Wrapped in Banana Leaf), Yum Kob Tam (Spicy Chicken Salad).

Coconut Cream Chicken Soup

Soup Dish | 20-minute Preparation | 25-minute Cooking | Serves 4

Ingredients

- 500 grams | 1 pound, 1½ ounces | 5 cups grated, peeled coconut
- 750 ml | 24 fl oz | 3 cups water
- 3 stalks lemon grass, bruised
- 6 kaffir lime leaves, torn into halves + 3 more leaves for garnishing
- 4 coriander roots, cut into 1-cm | ½-inch lengths
- 5 tablespoons fish sauce (*nam pla*)
- 100 grams | 3½ ounces fresh oyster mushrooms
- 500 grams | 1 pound, 1½ ounces chicken, cut into small pieces
- juice of 4 limes
- 1 tablespoon crushed palm sugar (jaggery) or brown sugar
- 10 bird's eye chillies
- 4 dried chillies, roasted and cut into small pieces
- powdered chilli

Method

1. Combine the coconut and water and extract 1 litre | 32 fl oz | 4 cups coconut milk. Bring the milk to a boil over low heat.
2. Add the lemon grass, kaffir lime leaves, coriander roots, fish sauce, oyster mushrooms and stir well. Add the chicken and cook until tender. Remove from heat.
3. Add the lime juice, palm sugar (jaggery) or brown sugar, bird's eye chillies and dried chillies and stir well.
4. Garnish with kaffir lime leaves and sprinkle with powdered chilli.

Gaeng Phed Kai
(Thai Chicken Curry)

Main Dish | 20-minute Preparation | 20-minute Cooking | Serves 4

Ingredients

- 1 portion boiled coconut cream (refer to page 78)
- 1 kilogram | 2 pounds, 3 ounces chicken, cut into small pieces
- 1 portion thin coconut milk (refer to page 78)
- 60 ml | 2 fl oz | ¼ cup fish sauce (*nam pla*)
- 4 large potatoes, peeled, boiled and quartered
- 1 red chilli
- coriander leaves (cilantro)
- radish, carved into flower shape

Finely Ground Paste

- 2.5 cm | 1 inch galangal, peeled
- 2 tablespoons coriander seeds, roasted
- 2 teaspoons cumin seeds, roasted
- 1 stalk lemon grass, sliced
- 10 dried chillies, seeded, soaked in hot water and drained
- 10 shallots, peeled
- 15 cloves garlic, peeled
- 5 cm | 2 inches ginger, peeled
- 2 teaspoons crushed dried shrimp paste
- 2 teaspoons salt

Method

1. Heat the boiled coconut cream for 5 minutes and stir-fry the finely ground paste until fragrant. Add the chicken and stir-fry well.
2. Pour in the thin coconut milk slowly, add the fish sauce, cover and cook until chicken is tender. Add the potatoes and bring to a boil.
3. Garnish with red chilli, coriander leaves (cilantro) and radish.

(From top) Coconut Cream Chicken Soup, Gaeng Phed Kai (Thai Chicken Curry).

Kai Haw Bai Toey
(Fried Chicken in Screwpine Leaf)

Main Dish | 25-minute Preparation |
20-minute Cooking | Serves 6

Ingredients

500 grams | 1 pound, 1¹/₂ ounces
    chicken fillet, cut into small pieces

1 tablespoon sugar

¹/₄ teaspoon monosodium glutamate

1 tablespoon sesame oil

2 tablespoons fish sauce (*nam pla*)

1 teaspoon dark soy sauce

15 screwpine leaves (*bai toey*)

500 ml | 16 fl oz | 2 cups cooking oil for
    deep-frying

Finely Ground Paste

4 cloves garlic, peeled

1 teaspoon ground white pepper

3 coriander roots, chopped

4 shallots, peeled

1 stalk lemon grass, sliced thinly

1 tablespoon preserved soy bean
    (*tau jiew*)

Method

1. Mix the chicken with the finely
   ground paste. Add sugar,
   monosodium glutamate, sesame oil,
   fish sauce, dark soy sauce and
   marinate for 30 minutes.
2. Wrap the marinated chicken in
   screwpine leaves.
3. Deep-fry for 10–12 minutes or until
   the screwpine leaves turn to dark
   green. Drain.

Kha Nom Beung Yooah
(Crisp-fried Pancakes with Chicken and Seafood Filling)

Side Dish | 20-minute Preparation |
30-minute Cooking | Serves 6

Ingredients

250 grams | 9 ounces | 1²/₃ cups plain
    (all-purpose) flour, sifted

2 duck eggs, beaten

1 tablespoon slaked lime, mixed with
    250 ml | 8 fl oz | 1 cup water

Chicken and Seafood Filling*

300 ml | 10 fl oz | 1¹/₄ cups cooking oil

lettuce leaves

onion, carved into flower shape

cucumber, carved into fan shape

radish, carved into leaf shape

Method

1. Combine the flour, eggs and lime
   water, a little at a time, and stir
   constantly until the batter becomes
   thick and creamy. Strain the batter.
2. Heat a non-stick frying pan (skillet)
   and pour 1 ladle of batter and make
   a pancake 5 cm / 2 inches wide and
   0.5 cm / ¹/₄ inch thick. Repeat until
   all the batter is used up.
3. Heat the cooking oil and deep-fry the
   pancakes, fold pancake into half
   with a skewer while frying. Drain.
4. Heap 1 tablespoon Chicken and
   Seafood Filling into pancake and top
   with lettuce slices.
5. Serve garnished with lettuce leaves,
   onion , cucumber and radish.

*Chicken and Seafood Filling

2 tablespoons cooking oil

140 grams | 5 ounces chicken fillet,
    coarsely minced (ground)

140 grams | 5 ounces shelled prawns
    (shrimps), coarsely minced (ground)

55 grams | 2 ounces crabmeat, shredded

45 grams | 1¹/₂ ounces preserved Chinese
    radish (*hua chai po*), finely diced

1 piece bean curd, finely diced and fried
    in 3 tablespoons cooking oil

2 tablespoons fish sauce (*nam pla*)

1 tablespoon sugar

2 kaffir lime leaves, finely chopped

70 grams | 2¹/₂ ounces bean sprouts,
    tailed, blanched and drained

45 grams | 1¹/₂ ounces | ¹/₃ cup roasted
    peanuts, coarsely pounded

salt

Finely Ground Paste

7 cloves garlic, peeled

15 black peppercorns

3 coriander roots

Method

1. Heat the cooking oil and sauté the
   finely ground paste until fragrant.
   Add the chicken, prawns (shrimps)
   and crabmeat and mix well.
2. Add the preserved Chinese radish,
   bean curd, fish sauce and sugar and
   stir-fry for 5 minutes.
3. Stir in the kaffir lime leaves, bean
   sprouts and peanuts.
4. Season with salt, remove from heat
   and set aside.

Chef's note: For the health conscious omit deep-frying the pancakes, simply fold in half and fill.

(From top) Kha Nom Beung Yooah (Crisp-fried Pancakes with Chicken and Seafood Filling), Kai Haw Bai Toey (Fried Chicken in Screwpine Leaf).

Ka Nom Jeen Nam Prik

(Noodles with Seafood and Vegetable Curry)

Noodle Dish | 20-minute Preparation |
20-minute Cooking | Serves 4–6

Ingredients

3 litres | 96 fl oz | 12 cups water

800 grams | 1³/₄ pounds dried thick rice noodles

2 portions thin coconut milk (refer to page 78)

700 grams | 1¹/₂ pounds prawns (shrimps)

280 grams | 10 ounces Spanish mackerel

125 ml | 4 fl oz | ¹/₂ cup fish sauce (*nam pla*)

200 grams | 7 ounces tamarind pulp

180 ml | 6 fl oz | ³/₄ cup water

2 tablespoons powdered chilli

200 grams | 7 ounces | 1¹/₈ cups crushed palm sugar (jaggery) or brown sugar

1 portion boiled coconut cream (refer to page 78)

red chilli strips

Pan-fried, Finely Ground Paste

15 dried chillies

10 shallots, peeled

10 cloves garlic, peeled

¹/₂ teaspoon grated kaffir lime rind

3.5 cm | 1¹/₂ inches galangal, peeled and thinly sliced

6 coriander roots

1 cm | ¹/₂ inch ginger, peeled

2.5 cm | 1 inch dried shrimp paste

Thickening Paste (blended)

125 ml | 4 fl oz | ¹/₂ cup water

125 grams | 4¹/₂ ounces | 1 cup ground, roasted peanuts

125 grams | 4¹/₂ ounces | 1 cup green pea flour (*tang mein*), sifted

Blanched Vegetables

200 grams | 7 ounces water convolvulus

200 grams | 7 ounces banana blossom (*dok kluai*), tough outer layers discarded, halved then cut into long strips

200 grams | 7 ounces long beans, cut into 5-cm | 2-inch lengths

200 grams | 7 ounces bean sprouts, tailed

Method

1. Boil 3 litres / 96 fl oz / 12 cups water, add the dried rice noodles and cook until soft. Drain and set aside.
2. Boil the thin coconut milk, prawns (shrimps) and fish for 10 minutes or until tender. Strain and reserve the stock. Shell the shrimps, de-bone the fish and grind together.
3. Combine the tamarind pulp and 180 ml / 6 fl oz / ³/₄ cup water and extract the juice.
4. Add fish sauce, tamarind juice, powdered chilli and palm sugar (jaggery) or brown sugar to the stock. Bring to a boil and keep aside.
5. Heat the boiled coconut cream for 5 minutes and fry the finely ground paste for 5 minutes until fragrant. Add the ground prawns and fish and the stock. Add thickening paste and cook for 10 minutes.
6. Serve rice noodles with blanched vegetables and pour curry on top. Garnish with red chilli strips.

Crunchy Fried Corn Cakes

Side Dish | 20-minute Preparation |
15-minute Cooking | Serves 4

Ingredients

450 grams | 1 pound | 2¹/₂ cups corn kernels

1 egg, beaten

1 teaspoon powdered turmeric

2 tablespoons rice flour

2 tablespoons light soy sauce

40 grams | 1¹/₂ ounces | ¹/₄ cup cornflour (cornstarch)

2 teaspoons salt

2 tablespoons chopped coriander leaves (cilantro)

280 grams | 10 ounces chicken fillet, chopped

3 tablespoons plain (all purpose) flour, sifted

500 ml | 16 fl oz | 2 cups cooking oil

Peanut and Cucumber Sauce*

1 tomato, peeled and form the peel into flower shape

green papaya, carved into leaf shape

Method

1. Combine corn kernels, egg, powdered turmeric, rice flour, light soy sauce, cornflour (cornstarch), salt, coriander leaves (cilantro) and chicken into a firm dough.
2. Shape the dough into round patties.
3. Dip the patties in the plain (all-purpose) flour and deep-fry until brown.
4. Garnish with tomato peel and green papaya and serve with Peanut and Cucumber Sauce.

*Peanut and Cucumber Sauce

125 ml | 4 fl oz | ¹/₂ cup vinegar

125 ml | 4 fl oz | ¹/₂ cup water

140 grams | 5 ounces | ²/₃ cup sugar

2 teaspoons salt

2 bird's eye chillies, coarsely pounded

3 tablespoons pounded, roasted peanuts

¹/₂ cucumber, thinly sliced

Method

1. Boil the vinegar, water, sugar, salt and bird's eye chillies. Cool.
2. Add the pounded peanuts and cucumber slices.

(Clockwise from top left) Blanched vegetables, Ka Nom Jeen Nam Prik (Noodles with Seafood and Vegetable Curry), Peanut and Cucumber Sauce, Crunchy Fried Corn Cakes.

Pra Ram Reong Sons
(Shredded Chicken and Vegetables with Peanut Sauce)

Main Dish | 30-minute Preparation | 15-minute Cooking | Serves 6

Ingredients

200 grams | 7 ounces chicken fillet

600 grams | 1 pound, 5 ounces water convolvulus

Peanut Sauce*

1 spring onion (scallion)

1 tomato, peeled and form the peel into flower

cucumber, carved into leaf shape

Method

1. Steam the chicken fillet and shred the meat. Keep aside.
2. Blanch the water convolvulus and drain thoroughly.
3. Arrange the vegetable on a serving dish, topped with shredded chicken and the Peanut Sauce.
4. Garnish with spring onion (scallion), tomato and cucumber.

*Peanut Sauce

3 tablespoons water

70 grams | 2¹/₂ ounces tamarind pulp

1 portion boiled coconut cream (refer to page 78)

150 grams | 5¹/₂ ounces red curry paste (*Nam Prik Gaeng Ped*, page 78)

2 coriander roots, chopped

1 portion thin coconut milk (refer page 78)

3 tablespoons fish sauce (*nam pla*)

2 tablespoons crushed palm sugar (jaggery) or brown sugar

140 grams | 5 ounces | 1 cup ground, roasted peanuts

Method

1. Combine the water and the tamarind pulp and extract the juice.
2. Heat the boiled coconut cream for 5 minutes, add the red curry paste and coriander roots and fry until fragrant.
3. Stir in the thin coconut milk, fish sauce, palm sugar (jaggery) or brown sugar, tamarind juice and peanuts. Cook until the gravy is slightly thick.

Kah Thong Thong
(Thai Pi Ti)

Side Dish | 30-minute Preparation | 25-minute Cooking | Serves 6

Ingredients

250 grams | 9 ounces | 2¹/₂ cups grated, peeled coconut

180 ml | 6 fl oz | ³/₄ cup water

85 grams | 3 ounces | ³/₄ cup plain flour (all-purpose), sifted

85 grams | 3 ounces | ¹/₂ cup rice flour, sifted

45 grams | 1¹/₂ ounces | ¹/₃ cup tapioca flour, sifted

1¹/₂ egg yolks

¹/₂ teaspoon salt

2 tablespoons crushed palm sugar (jaggery) or brown sugar

¹/₄ teaspoon slaked lime, mixed with 2 tablespoons water

1.25 litres | 40 fl oz | 5 cups cooking oil

Pai Ti Filling*

2 red chillies, finely sliced

lettuce leaves

pumpkin, carved into flower shape

Method

1. Squeeze the coconut and water and extract 180 ml / 6 fl oz / ³/₄ cup coconut milk.
2. Combine the plain flour (all-purpose), rice flour, tapioca flour, egg yolks, coconut milk, salt, palm sugar (jaggery) or brown sugar and lime water and mix to form a thick and creamy batter.
3. Heat the cooking oil and dip the *pai ti* mould in the oil for about 5 minutes to preheat.
4. Dip the *pai ti* mould in the batter and deep-fry until golden brown. Drain and set aside to cool. Repeat with the remaining batter.
5. To serve, put some of the lettuce and filling into the *pai ti* casings and top with red chillies. Garnish with lettuce leaves and pumpkin.

*Pai Ti Filling

2 tablespoons cooking oil

280 grams | 10 ounces small prawns (shrimps), shelled, deveined and diced

280 grams | 10 ounces chicken fillet, diced

140 grams | 5 ounces | ³/₄ cup corn kernels

3 tablespoons fish sauce (*nam pla*)

2 tablespoons sugar

110 grams | 4 ounces coriander leaves (cilantro), cut into 1-cm | ¹/₂-inch lengths

1 tablespoon cornflour (cornstarch), blended with 2 tablespoons water

Finely Ground Paste

3 coriander roots

10 cloves garlic, peeled

15 white peppercorns

Method

1. Heat the cooking oil and sauté the finely ground paste until fragrant.
2. Add the prawns (shrimps), chicken, corn kernels, fish sauce and sugar and stir-fry for about 5 minutes or until dry.
3. Add the coriander leaves (cilantro) and mix well. Stir in the cornflour (cornstarch) mixture to thicken the sauce. Set aside to cool.

Chef's note: *Pai ti* moulds are available in Oriental shops.

(From top) Pra Ram Reong Sons (Shredded Chicken and Vegetable with Peanut Sauce), Kah Thong Thong (Thai Pai Ti).

Siamese Laksa

Noodle Dish | 30-minute Preparation |
20-minute Cooking | Serves 6

Ingredients

800 grams | 1³/4 pounds Indian Mackerel fish

700 grams | 1¹/2 pounds | 7 cups grated, peeled coconut

2.25 litres | 72 fl oz | 9 cups water

125 ml | 4 fl oz | ¹/2 cup cooking oil

800 grams | 1³/4 pounds yellow noodles, blanched and drained just before serving

Finely Ground Paste

60 grams | 2 ounces | ¹/4 cup ground chillies

15 shallots, peeled

3 stalks lemon grass, sliced

5 cm | 2 inches galangal, peeled

2.5 cm | 1 inch turmeric, peeled

2.5 cm | 1 inch dried shrimp paste

3 kaffir lime leaves

8 cloves garlic, peeled

1 teaspoon ground black pepper

6 candlenuts

Garnish

400 grams | 14 ounces peeled pineapple, cut into strips

400 grams | 14 ounces cucumber, cut into thin strips

100 grams | 3¹/2 ounces mint leaves

100 grams | 3¹/2 ounces bean sprouts, tailed, blanched and drained just before serving

70 grams | 2¹/2 ounces Chinese chives, cut into 1.25-cm | ¹/2-inch lengths

1 large onion, peeled and sliced into rings

Method

1. Clean and gut the fish. Steam for 10 minutes and shred. Set aside.
2. Mix the grated coconut with water and extract 2.5 litres / 80 fl oz / 10 cups coconut milk.
3. Heat the cooking oil and fry the finely ground paste until fragrant.
4. Add the coconut milk and boil until it separates, stir constantly to prevent the milk from curdling.
5. Add the shredded fish and cook for another 5 minutes.
6. Place some of the blanched noodles in a bowl, pour the gravy on top and add a small amount of each of the garnish ingredients. Serve hot.

Tod Man Pla
(Spicy Red Curry Fish Cake)

Side Dish | 25-minute Preparation |
25-minute Cooking | Serves 6

Ingredients

140 grams | 5 ounces red curry paste (*Nam Prik Gaeng Ped*, page 78)

500 grams | 1 pound, 1¹/2 ounces red snapper fillet, minced (ground)

1 small (70 grams | 2¹/2 ounce) egg, beaten

3 tablespoons fish sauce (*nam pla*)

1 sprig coriander leaves (cilantro), chopped

1 tablespoon crushed palm sugar (jaggery) or brown sugar

80 grams | 2³/4 ounces long beans, thinly sliced

750 ml | 24 fl oz | 3 cups cooking oil

Chilli Sauce*

Method

1. Combine the red curry paste and minced (ground) fish with the egg, fish sauce, coriander leaves (cilantro), palm sugar (jaggery) or brown sugar, long beans and knead into a soft dough.
2. Shape 2 tablespoons of the dough into a ball and flatten slightly. Deep-fry the fish cakes until golden brown. Drain. Serve with Chilli Sauce.

*Chilli Sauce

200 grams | 7 ounces | 1 cup sugar

2 teaspoons salt

125 ml | 4 fl oz | ¹/2 cup vinegar

2 tablespoons water

5 cloves garlic, peeled and finely ground

2 red chillies, finely ground

3 shallots, peeled and sliced

1 cucumber, quartered lengthways and thinly sliced

3 tablespoons pounded, roasted peanuts

Method

1. Boil sugar, salt, vinegar and water until sugar dissolved.
2. Add the garlic, red chillies, shallots, cucumber slices, peanuts and mix well.

Chef's note: Spanish mackerel can be substituted for red snapper.
This sauce can be garnished with coriander leaves (cilantro).

(Clockwise from top left) Vegetables for garnishing, Siamese Laksa, Tod Man Pla (Spicy Red Curry Fish Cake), Chilli Sauce.

Kao Tom Pad
(Steamed Glutinous Rice with Banana and Kidney Beans)

Dessert Dish | 20-minute Preparation |
30-minute Cooking | Serves 6

Ingredients

500 grams | 1 pound, 1¹/₂ ounces | 5 cups grated, peeled coconut

750 ml | 24 fl oz | 3 cups water

1 teaspoon salt

125 grams | 4¹/₂ ounces | ¹/₂ cup sugar

450 grams | 1 pound | 2 cups glutinous rice, washed, soaked in water for about 3–4 hours and drained

5 banana leaves, cut into 10 x 15-cm | 4 x 6-inch pieces

2 semi-ripe bananas, peeled and finely sliced

125 grams | 4¹/₂ ounces | ³/₄ cup kidney beans, washed and boiled until soft

Method

1. Combine the coconut and water and extract the milk.
2. Add the salt and sugar to the coconut milk and stir well until the sugar has dissolved. Strain the coconut milk through a muslin cloth.
3. Bring to a boil and add the glutinous rice. Stir constantly over medium heat until the liquid is absorbed. Remove from heat and set aside to cool.
4. Place 1 tablespoon of the glutinous rice on a piece of banana leaf and flatten the rice slightly. Layer with a few slices of banana, another tablespoonful of glutinous rice and some kidney beans. Roll up the banana leaf and fold the ends together. Repeat until all the ingredients are used up.
5. Steam over rapidly boiling water for about 20–25 minutes.

Khanom Bah Bin
(Coconut Cake)

Dessert Dish | 10-minute Preparation |
20-minute Cooking | Serves 4

Ingredients

2 eggs

200 grams | 7 ounces | 2 cups flaked (hand grated), peeled coconut

310 grams | 11 ounces | 1¹/₂ cups sugar

75 grams | 2¹/₂ ounces | ²/₃ cup glutinous rice flour, sifted

35 grams | 1¹/₄ ounces | ¹/₄ cup arrowroot flour, sifted

1 teaspoon vanilla essence

2 egg yolks, beaten

Method

1. Combine the eggs, coconut flakes, sugar, glutinous rice flour, arrowroot flour and vanilla essence to form a creamy batter.
2. Grease 15-cm / 6-inch fluted muffin tins. Spoon the batter into the tins and top with the beaten egg yolks.
3. Bake in a preheated 180°C / 350°F oven for 20 minutes or until golden. Cool completely before removing from the tin.

Chef's note: The cake may also be baked in a 15 x 15-cm / 6 x 6-inch cake tin for 25 minutes.

(From top) Khanom Bah Bin (Coconut Cake), Kao Tom Pad (Steamed Glutinous Rice with Banana and Kidney Beans).

Tak Koa Med Bou
(Water Chestnut Cake with Coconut Cream Topping)

Dessert Dish | 20-minute Preparation | 20-minute Cooking | Serves 6

Ingredients

- 5 heaped tablespoons arrowroot flour, sifted
- 3 tablespoons screwpine leaf (*bay toey*) juice (refer to page 78)
- 750 ml | 24 fl oz | 3 cups water
- 220 grams | 8 ounces | 1 cup sugar
- 12 water chestnuts, peeled and finely diced
- 30 screwpine leaves (*bay toey*) cases
- Coconut Cream Topping*

Method

1. Cook the arrowroot flour, screwpine leaf juice, water and sugar until thick and shiny. Add in the chestnuts and mix well. Pour into screwpine leaf cases (half-filled). Set in the refrigerator for about 30 minutes.
2. Fill with the Coconut Cream Topping and leave aside to cool.

*Coconut Cream Topping

- 500 grams | 1 pound, 1 1/2 ounces | 5 cups grated, peeled coconut
- 560 ml | 18 fl oz | 2 1/4 cups water
- 2 tablespoons rice flour, sifted
- 1 tablespoon cornflour (cornstarch), sifted
- 1/2 teaspoon salt

Method

1. Combine the grated coconut and water and extract 625 ml / 20 fl oz / 2 1/2 cups coconut milk.
2. Cook the coconut milk with the rice flour, cornflour (cornstarch) and salt until thick.

Thab Thim Grob
(Pomegranate Seeds in Coconut Milk)

Dessert Dish | 10-minute Preparation | 25-minute Cooking | Serves 6

Ingredients

- 300 grams | 10 1/2 ounces water chestnuts, peeled and finely diced
- 1 teaspoon red food colouring, dissolved in 250 ml | 8 fl oz | 1 cup water
- 60 grams | 2 ounces | 1/2 cup tapioca flour, sifted
- 2 tablespoons cornflour (cornstarch), sifted
- 1.15 litres | 37 fl oz | 4 1/2 cups water
- Coconut Syrup*

Method

1. Soak water chestnut cubes in coloured water until they turn red.
2. Combine the tapioca flour and cornflour (cornstarch). Roll the water chestnut cubes in the flour to coat. Shake off excess flour.
3. Bring the water to a boil. Add the coated water chestnut cubes and boil for 3 minutes. Remove and rinse under running water. Drain well.
4. Wrap the cooked water chestnut cubes in thin muslin cloth and set aside.
5. To serve, top water chestnut cubes with coconut syrup and shaved ice.

*Coconut Syrup

- 250 grams | 9 ounces | 2 1/2 cups grated, peeled coconut
- 460 ml | 14 3/4 fl oz | 1 4/5 cups water
- 150 grams | 5 1/2 ounces | 3/4 cup sugar
- 2 screwpine leaves (*bay toey*), shredded and knotted

Method

1. Combine the coconut and 250 ml / 8 fl oz / 1 cup water to extract 300 ml / 10 fl oz / 1 1/4 cups coconut milk. Set aside.
2. Boil the sugar, the remaining water and screwpine leaves. Remove and set aside to cool.
3. Add the coconut milk and stir well.

(From top) Tak Koa Med Bou (Water Chesnut Cake with Coconut Cream Topping), Thab Thim Grob (Pomegranate Seeds in Coconut Milk).

Khanom Chan
(Steamed Layer Cake)

Dessert Dish | 30-minute Preparation |
20-minute Cooking | Serves 4

Ingredients

600 grams | 1 pound, 5 ounces |
  2³/₄ cups sugar

250 ml | 8 fl oz | 1 cup jasmine-scented
  water (refer to page 78)

260 grams | 9 ounces | 2 cups arrowroot
  flour, sifted

35 grams | 1¹/₄ ounces | ¹/₄ cup rice flour,
  sifted

75 grams | 2¹/₂ ounces | ²/₃ cup tapioca
  flour, sifted

310 ml | 10 fl oz | 1¹/₄ cup thick coconut
  milk (refer to page 78)

1 portion thin coconut milk
  (refer to page 78)

60 ml | 2 fl oz | ¹/₄ cup screwpine leaf
  (*bay toey*) juice (refer to page 78)

3 drops green food colouring

Method

1. Boil sugar and jasmine-scented
   water into syrup, allow to cool.
2. Mix the arrowroot flour, rice flour
   and tapioca flour. Add 250 ml / 8 fl
   oz / 1 cup thick coconut milk and
   cooled syrup. Mix until well blended
   and smooth.
3. Add the thin coconut milk, mix well
   and strain twice.
4. Divide the batter into two equal
   parts. To one part, add the remaining
   thick coconut milk. To the other
   part, add the screwpine leaf juice,
   and food colouring.
5. Grease a 20-cm / 8-inch square cake
   tin with vegetable oil and preheat in
   a steamer for 5 minutes.
6. Pour 5 tablespoons of green batter
   and steam for 3 minutes.
7. Layer with 5 tablespoons of plain
   batter and steam for another 3
   minutes.
8. Repeat the procedure, alternating
   the plain and green batter. End with
   a layer of green batter and steam for
   5 minutes. Dry the moisture that
   forms on top of each layer before
   adding the next layer.
9. Cool completely before cutting.

Khanom Rae Rai
(Steamed Rice Vermicelli with Coconut Topping)

Dessert Dish | 45-minute Preparation |
20-minute Cooking | Serves 4

Ingredients

300 grams | 10¹/₂ ounces | 2¹/₂ cups rice
  flour, sifted

35 grams | 1¹/₄ ounces | ¹/₄ cup
  arrowroot flour, sifted

310 ml | 10 fl oz | 1¹/₄ cups jasmine-
  scented water (refer to page 78)

250 ml | 8 fl oz | 1 cup thick coconut
  milk (refer to page 78)

food colouring

banana leaves, cut into 7.5-cm | 3-inch
  squares and lightly greased

Coconut Topping*

55 grams | 2 ounces | ¹/₂ cup toasted
  sesame seeds

Method

1. Mix rice flour and arrowroot flour.
2. Combine jasmine-scented water with
   125 ml / 4 fl oz / ¹/₂ cup thick
   coconut milk and pour into the flour
   mixture, mix to a smooth
   consistency.
3. Cook the batter on a medium heat
   until elastic in texture. Remove from
   the heat. Add the remaining thick
   coconut milk to the batter and knead
   into a dough.
4. Divide the dough into four equal
   portions and colour each a different
   shade.
5. Use a vermicelli press or *muruku*
   mould and form mounds of rice
   vermicelli strips with dough on the
   banana leaf squares. Repeat with the
   other portions of coloured dough.
6. Steam over rapid boiling water for
   10 minutes.
7. Sprinkle Coconut Topping and
   sesame seeds on the steamed rice
   vermicelli.

*Coconut Topping

125 grams | 4¹/₂ ounces | 1¹/₄ cups
  grated, peeled coconut

125 grams | 4¹/₂ ounces | ¹/₂ cup sugar

¹/₄ teaspoon salt

Method

Combine all the ingredients. Set aside.

Chef's note: This dessert can be served with
boiled coconut cream (refer to page 78).

(From top) Khanom Chan (Steamed Layer Cake), Khanom Rae Rai (Steamed Rice Vermicelli with Coconut Topping).

Stock, Curry Paste, Flavouring and Coconut Milk

Chicken Stock

Stock | 10-minute Preparation |
2–3-hour Cooking | 1 Portion

3 kilograms | 6 pounds, 9 ounces chicken carcass
5 litres | 160 fl oz | 20 cups water
200 grams | 7 ounces celery stalks, cut into 1.5-cm | $^3/_4$-inch pieces
2 teaspoons peppercorns, coarsely pounded
5 cm | 2 inches galangal, sliced
1 tablespoon salt
4 large onions, quartered

1. Simmer all the ingredients in a stock pot over a medium heat for 2–3 hours until the stock is reduced to 4 litres / 128 fl oz / 16 cups.
2. Strain through muslin cloth, divide into required portions and store in containers. The stock can be kept frozen for 3 months.

Nam Prik Gaeng Keo Wan

(Green Curry Paste)

Basic Curry Paste | 15-minute
Preparation | 1 Portion

1.5 cm | $^3/_4$ inch dried shrimp paste
$^1/_2$ teaspoon grated kaffir lime rind
$^1/_2$ teaspoon cumin seeds
$^1/_4$ teaspoon grated nutmeg
1 teaspoon sugar
2 teaspoons coriander seeds
5 cm | 2 inches galangal, peeled
2.5 cm | 1 inch turmeric, peeled
1 tablespoon chopped coriander root
170 grams | 6 ounces | $^3/_4$ cup chopped lemon grass
40 bird's eye chillies
20 white peppercorns
7 cloves garlic, peeled
seeds of 6 cardamoms
6 shallots, peeled

Grind or blend all the ingredients to a fine paste.

Nam Prik Gaeng Ped

(Red Curry Paste)

Basic Curry Paste | 15-minute
Preparation | 1 Portion

1 tablespoon coriander seeds
1 teaspoon cumin seeds
2.5 cm | 1 inch dried shrimp paste
1 teaspoon chopped kaffir lime rind
20 white peppercorns
15 dried chillies, seeded, soak in hot water and drained
10 shallots, peeled
55 grams | 2 ounces peeled garlic
2.5 cm | 1 inch galangal, peeled
2 stalks lemon grass, thinly sliced
2 coriander roots

1. Pan-fry the coriander and cumin seeds for 5 minutes and grind into a powder.
2. Blend the remaining ingredients to a fine paste. Add the powdered cumin and coriander and mix well.
3. Divide into required portions and store in containers. Refrigerate for future use.

Chef's note: Red curry paste is a basic curry paste that can be used for other dishes, e.g. fish cake, fish paste, chicken, meat or seafood.

Nam Prik Gaeng Mussaman

(Mussaman Curry Paste)

Basic Curry Paste | 20-minute
Preparation | 1 Portion

2 cloves garlic, peeled
1.5 cm | $^3/_4$ inch galangal, peeled
1 stalk lemon grass, thinly sliced
5 shallots, peeled
1 tablespoon coriander seeds
1 teaspoon cumin seeds
5 black peppercorns
1 cm | $^1/_2$ inch dried shrimp paste
8 dried chillies, seeded, soaked in hot water and drained

1. Pan-fry all the ingredients except dried chillies for 5 minutes.
2. Grind or blend together all the ingredients to a fine paste.
3. Store in an airtight containers. It can be kept frozen for 1–2 months.

Nam Prik Pau

(All-purpose Roasted Chilli Paste)

Basic Curry Paste | 35-minute
Preparation | 30-minute Cooking |
1 Portion

750 ml | 24 fl oz | 3 cups vegetable oil
280 grams | 10 ounces peeled shallots, sliced
280 grams | 10 ounces peeled garlic, sliced
280 grams | 10 ounces | $1^7/_8$ cups dried prawns (shrimps), soaked in water and drained
2.5 cm | 1 inch dried shrimp paste, roasted and crushed
170 grams | 6 ounces dried chillies, seeded, soaked in water and drained
140 grams | 5 ounces | $^3/_4$ cup crushed palm sugar (jaggery) or brown sugar
60 ml | 2 fl oz | $^1/_4$ cup fish sauce (*nam pla*)
60 ml | 2 fl oz | $^1/_4$ cup tamarind juice, extracted from 2 tablespoons tamarind pulp and 60 ml | 2 fl oz | $^1/_4$ cup water
2 teaspoons salt
2 teaspoons monosodium glutamate

1. Heat the vegetable oil and fry the shallots and garlic until golden brown, remove from oil and drain.
2. In the same oil, fry the dried prawns (shrimps), shrimp paste and chillies for 3 minutes until golden brown and fragrant. Cool the oil.
3. Grind the dried prawns (shrimps), shrimp paste, chillies, shallots, garlic and palm sugar (jaggery) or brown sugar to a fine paste.
4. Add the fish sauce, tamarind juice, salt, monosodium glutamate and the cooled oil. Blend again to obtain a fine textured paste. Store in an airtight bottle.

Chef's note: This paste is extremely versatile. It can be used for cooking vegetables, chicken and meat or to marinate fish. It enhances the flavour of soups. If properly fried and stored, the paste can be kept for a few of months.

Screwpine Leaf Water

Flavouring | 15-minute Preparation |
1 Portion

10 screwpine leaves (*bay toey*)
3 tablespoons water

1. Cut the screwpine leaves crosswise into 2.5-cm / 1-inch lengths.
2. Pound the leaves, add water and squeeze to extract the juice. Strain the juice through muslin cloth.

Coconut Cream

Coconut Cream | 5-minute
Preparation | 1 Portion

1 mature coconut, peeled and grated

Squeeze the grated coconut without water, using muslin cloth, to obtain thick coconut cream.

Thick and Thin Coconut Milk

Coconut Milk | 10-minute
Preparation | 1 Portion

500 grams | 1 pound, $1^1/_2$ ounces | 5 cups grated, peeled coconut
680 ml | $22^2/_3$ fl oz | $2^2/_3$ cups water

1. Combine grated coconut and 180 ml / 6 fl oz / $^3/_4$ cup water. Squeeze and extract 250 ml / 8 fl oz / 1 cup thick coconut milk.
2. Add 500 ml / 16 fl oz / 2 cups water to the coconut and extract thin coconut milk.

Boiled Coconut Cream

Boiled Coconut Cream | 5-minute
Preparation | 20-minute Cooking |
1 Portion

500 grams | 1 pound, $1^1/_2$ ounces | 5 cups grated, peeled coconut
435 ml | 14 fl oz | $1^3/_4$ cups water

1. Combine water and grated coconut, squeeze and extract coconut milk.
2. Boil the coconut milk until it separates and milk is reduced to 250 ml / 8 fl oz / 1 cup.

Jasmine-scented Water

Flavouring | 1 Portion

30 grams | 1 ounce jasmine flowers
1 litre | 32 fl oz | 4 cups water

Soak the jasmine flowers in water overnight. Strain and store in container. Keep the water in the refrigerator. It can keep for 1 month.

Chef's note: If you do not like like smell of jasmine, just use water in your recipe.

1. Nam Prik Gaeng Mussaman (Mussaman Curry Paste). 2. Scented slaked lime. 3. Boiled Coconut Cream. 4. Nam Prik Pau (All-purpose Roasted Chilli Paste).
5. Nam Prik Gaeng Keo Wan (Green Curry Paste). 6. Screwpine Leaf Water. 7. Nam Phrik Gaeng Ped (Red Curry Paste).

Sauces & Dips

Nam Prik Pla
(Fish and Chilli Sauce Dip)

Dipping Sauce | 25-minute
Preparation | 1 Portion

5–6 bird's eye chillies
5 shallots with skin
3 cloves garlic with skin
125 ml | 4 fl oz | 1/2 cup water
**1.5 cm | 3/4 inch dried shrimp
paste**
**200 grams | 7 ounces Indian
mackerel or sole fillet**
3 tablespoons lime juice
3 tablespoons fish sauce (nam pla)
**1 tablespoon crushed palm sugar
(jaggery) or brown sugar**
1 spring onion (scallion), chopped
**1 sprig coriander leaves (cilantro),
chopped**

1. Pan-fry the bird's eye chillies, shallots, garlic and shrimp paste for 5 minutes.
2. Peel the shallots and garlic and grind with bird's eye chillies.
3. Boil the water, add the shrimp paste and fish fillet and cook until the fish is tender.
4. Remove the fish and pound with the shallots, garlic and chillies until all the ingredients are ground to a fine paste.
5. Strain the fish broth and add the paste to the broth. Add the lime juice, fish sauce and palm sugar (jaggery) or brown sugar and mix well. Add water if a thin sauce is needed.
6. Garnish with spring onions (scallions) and coriander leaves (cilantro).
7. Serve with blanched vegetables or grilled (broiled) fish.

Nam Prik Kapi
(Shrimp Paste and Chilli Dip)

Dipping Sauce | 20-minute
Preparation | 1 Portion

2.5 cm | 1 inch dried shrimp paste
**4 cloves garlic, peeled and
chopped**
**1 tablespoon dried prawns
(shrimps), soaked in water and
drained**
**1/2 tablespoon chopped, peeled
lesser ginger (kra chai)**
8 bird's eye chillies
3 tablespoons lemon juice
3 tablespoons fish sauce (nam pla)
**1 tablespoon crushed palm sugar
(jaggery) or brown sugar**
1 tablespoon sliced pea eggplant

1. Pound or blend the shrimp paste, garlic, dried prawns (shrimps), lesser ginger and bird's eye chillies until fine.
2. Add the lemon juice, fish sauce, palm sugar (jaggery) or brown sugar and pea eggplant.
3. Serve with any cooked vegetables or with grilled (broiled) fish.

Sticky Chilli Sauce

Dipping Sauce | 20-minute Preparation |
5-minute Cooking | 1 Portion

Ingredients

250 ml | 8 fl oz | 1 cup vinegar
**250 grams | 9 ounces | 1 1/8 cups
sugar**
salt
2 tablespoons liquid glucose

Finely Ground Paste

2 red chillies
1 yellow bird's eye chilli
10 cloves garlic, peeled

1. Combine the vinegar, sugar and salt and bring to a boil.
2. Add the finely ground paste and cook on a low heat for about 5 minutes.
3. Add the glucose and stir well. Cool.

Lon Tau Jiew
(Coconut Milk and Preserved
Soy Bean Sauce Dip)

Dipping Sauce | 35-minute
Preparation | 20-minute Cooking |
1 Portion

300 ml | 10 fl oz | 1 1/4 cups water
**300 grams | 10 1/2 ounces |
3 cups grated, peeled coconut**
**110 grams | 4 ounces preserved
soy bean paste (tau jiew nam)**
2 shallots, peeled
2 shallots, peeled and thinly sliced
**125 grams | 4 1/2 ounces finely
chopped shelled shrimps
(prawns)**
**125 grams | 4 1/2 ounces
finely chopped chicken fillet**
4 red chillies, finely shredded
**3 tablespoons crushed palm sugar
(jaggery) or brown sugar**
**3 tablespoons thick tamarind
juice, extracted from 2
tablespoons tamarind pulp and
3 tablespoons water**
**1 sprig coriander leaves (cilantro),
cut into 1-cm | 1/2-inch lengths**
1 red chilli, seeded and diced

1. Add the water to the coconut and extract 500 ml / 16 fl oz / 2 cups thick coconut milk.
2. Boil the coconut milk in a frying pan (skillet) until it separates to become boiled coconut cream.
3. Pound the preserved soy bean paste and the 2 shallots to a fine paste.
4. Add to the boiled coconut cream and stir well.
5. Add the shrimps (prawns), chicken, shallot slices, red chillies, palm sugar (jaggery) or brown sugar and tamarind juice. Stir constantly and bring to a boil.
6. Remove from heat and garnish with coriander (cilantro) leaves and red chillies.
7. Serve with fresh vegetables.

Sweet and Sour Sauce

Dipping Sauce | 10-minute
Preparation | 1 Portion

**4 bird's eye chillies, finely
chopped**
**7 cloves garlic, peeled and finely
chopped**
**250 grams | 9 ounces | 1 1/8 cups
sugar**
**2 salted pickled plums, stoned
and finely chopped**
2 teaspoons salt
125 ml | 4 fl oz | 1/2 cup vinegar

Combine all the ingredients and mix well.

Nam Prik Noom
(Green Chilli Dip)

Dipping Sauce | 25-minute
Preparation | 15-minute Cooking |
1 Portion

120 ml | 4 fl oz | 1/2 cup cooking oil
**2 tablespoons chopped dried
salted mackerel fish**
**20 green chillies, coarsely
chopped and roasted**
**20 cloves garlic, peeled, coarsely
chopped and roasted**
**12 shallots, peeled and coarsely
chopped**
1 tomato, diced
2 tablespoons hot water
**2 tablespoons chopped spring
onions (scallions)**
**2 tablespoons chopped coriander
leaves (cilantro)**
**90 ml | 3 fl oz | 3/8 cup fish sauce
(nam pla)**

1. Heat the cooking oil in a frying pan and fry the salted fish over a medium heat until brown. Drain thoroughly.
2. Blend the fish with green chillies, garlic, shallots and tomatoes to a rough consistency.
3. Add hot water, spring onions (scallions), coriander leaves (cilantro) and fish sauce.

Chef's note: This dip may be served with raw cabbage, sliced cucumber and fried fish.

1. Nam Prik Noom (Green Chilli Dip). 2. Nam Prik Kapi (Shrimp Paste and Chilli Dip). 3. Sticky Chilli Sauce. 4. Sweet and Sour Sauce.
5. Lon Tau Jiew (Coconut Milk and Preserved Soy Bean Sauce Dip). 6. Nam Prik Pla (Fish and Chilli Sauce Dip).

Glossary

Basil (*Ocimum spp.*)

Asian basil also known as sweet basil is used widely in Thailand. Several varieties are used to flavour foods. The sweet aromatic fragrance of *bai horapa* graces many dishes. *Maenglak* or lemon basil is used in soups. Basil leaves are best used fresh, they do not retain their flavour when dried.

Banana blossom (*Musa spp.*)

Dok kluai in Thai, it is also called 'banana heart' as its shape is similar to a cow's heart and it is found at the end of banana fruit bunch. The tough outer layers must be removed until the yellow part is exposed. This part can be finely cubed and cooked with spices or blanched and eaten with sauce dip.

Bean curd

Made from soy beans, there are several types ranging from soft white (*tau huu khaao chanit awn*) to small hard squares (*tau huu leuang*). The soft bean curd is used in soup while the hard variety is used in fried dishes.

Butterfly / Blue pea flowers (*Clitoria ternatea*)

Anjan in Thai, this tropical, slender twiner has dark bluish purple showy flowers. The flowers can be boiled with a little water to obtain a blue colour solution that can be used to colour desserts. The seeds and roots are used in India as a laxative and diuretic.

Chilli (*Capsicum frutescens*)

Chillies are generally known as *prik* and are used extensively in Thai cooking. Several varieties are available ranging from green (unripe) and red (ripe) to yellow (*prik chee*). Red chillies dried in the sun are called *prik haeng*, pounded in to flakes they are called *prik pone*. The hottest chilli is the tiny bird's eye chilli (*prik khee noo*). Chillies may be adjusted to suit individual taste.

Chinese chives (*Allium tuberosum*)

Known as *ku chai* in Thai, Chinese chives have thick, narrow, flat leaves much like a spring onion (scallion) and has a stronger flavour than the Western chives.

Coconut (*Cocos nucifera*)

The use of coconut (*maprao*) in many forms is a hallmark of Thai cooking. Coconut milk is the liquid extracted by soaking fresh, grated coconut in water and then straining it. Coconut milk may be either thick or thin. It is best to use fresh, grated coconut whenever possible, substitute packaged coconut if it is not available.

Coriander (*Coriandrum sativum*)

Coriander is probably the most common ingredient used in Thai cooking after chillies. Commonly known as cilantro or Chinese parsley, it is called *phak chee* in Thai. The plant is fully edible. The leaves are used to flavour and garnish foods. The roots are pounded with garlic and peppercorns to be used as basic seasoning. The seeds have a pleasant taste and fragrance and are indispensable when making a curry.

Eggplant

Also known as aubergine or brinjal, the eggplant comes in a variety of shapes, sizes and flavours. Pea eggplants (*Solanum torvum*), known as *makhua puang* in Thai, grow in clusters and are used in curry preparations. Garden eggplants (*Solanum melongena*), called *makhua*

yao in Thai range from small spheres of white to the long, slender, purple variety.

Fish sauce

This clear brown liquid made from a brew of fermented fish or prawns (shrimps) mixed with salt is known as *nam pla* in Thai. Fish sauce is commonly used to flavour foods during cooking and it is served as a condiment, either by itself or spiked with sliced chillies and sometimes lime juice.

Galangal

Galangal is a rhizome similar to the ginger family. Greater galangal (*Alpinia galanga*), known as *kha* in Thai lends its distinctive taste to enhance various dishes. Preferably used fresh, galangal is also available in dried and powdered form.

Ginger (*Zingiber officinale*)

Known as *khing* in Thai, only the fresh variety is used for cooking. Young ginger is juicier than the mature variety. Peel the skin of mature variety before cooking. Lesser ginger (*Kaempferia panduratum*) known as *kra chai* in Thai, appears in bunches of slender and short tuberous roots, brown in colour and with a mild flavour. It can be omitted if unavailable.

Jasmine (*Jasminum sambac*)

Jasmin water, obtained by soaking the flowers (*malee*) in water, adds fragrance to Thai desserts and cakes. Bottled essence can be used as substitute.

Kaffir lime (*Citrus hystrix, C. papedia*)

Also known as leprous lime, it is known as *makrut* in Thai. This knobbly, wrinkled citrus fruit has a fragrant skin and virtually no juice, the grated rind is added to food and its leaves (*bai makrut*) are used in curries and soups.

Kalamansi / Musk lime (*Citrus microcarpa, C. mitis*)

This is a small variety of lime which is more fragrant than its counterpart. If can be substituted with half-ripe kumquats or lemon.

Lemon grass (*Cymbopogon citratus*)

Lemon grass or *takrai* in Thai, is an aromatic grey-green grass that grown in clumps. Only the lower portion of the stem, the bottom 10–15 cm is used for cooking. If it is to be blended into a paste only the tender centre is used, the outer layer is discarded. Lemon grass has a distinctive lemony flavour and is used in many Thai dishes.

Mushrooms

Mushrooms both fresh and dried are used in Thai cooking. The dried black variety—Chinese or shiitake—is used most commonly. Dried mushrooms should be soaked for 20 minutes in warm water before use.

Palm sugar

Also known as jaggery, palm sugar is made from the sap of coconut or palmyra palm (*Borassus flabellifera*). It varies in colour from gold to light brown, is less sweet than cane sugar and has a distinctive flavour and fragrance. Commonly known as *nam taan pep, nam taan bik, nam taan mapraow*, palm sugar is used in both savoury and sweet dishes in Thailand. If unavailable, use soft brown sugar mixed with a bit of golden syrup.

Pearl Sago

It is made from the flour which comes from the trunks of sago palm (*metroxylon rumphii, m sagu*). Commonly shaped into pellets, wet sago flour is pressed through a seive and dried on a hot surface. These white pellets will turn transparent when cooked.

Pointed pepper leaves (*Piper samentosum*)

Known in Thai as *cha plu* and *daun kaduk* in Malay, this creeper has aromatic, glossy, dark green leaves. It can be omitted if unavailable.

Shrimp paste

Shrimp paste is used extensively in Thai cooking. It is known as *kapi* in Thailand, *belacan* in Malaysia and Singapore and *terasi* in Indonesia. This fine textured paste ranges in colour from pink to black-brown and should be cooked before eating. If the recipe does not specify that it should be fried with other ingredients, it is best to grill or pan-fry the paste before pounding. Shrimp paste is commonly used in curry preparations and in dipping sauces.

Screwpine leaf (*Pandanus amaryllifolius*)

Commonly known as pandan leaf or *bai toey* in Thai, the delicate flavour of the screwpine leaf is used to enhance many Asian dishes. Seasoned meat wrapped in the leaf acquires exactly this flavour. Essence is extracted from the leaf and is used to flavour cakes and desserts. Bottled essence can be used as substitute.

Slaked lime

A type of white substance obtained by burning and grinding cockle shells until fine. It is normally eaten with betel leaves.

Sponge Gourd (*Luffa acutangula*)

Known as *buap liam* in Thai, it is an oblong, pointed dark green gourd which has sharp longitudinal ridges. It is also know as four-angled loofah.

Tamarind (*Tamarindus indica*)

Tamarind or *ma khaam* in Thai is used in many Thai preparations. Tamarind juice is used to impart a fragrant sourness to foods. The pulp is soaked in water for 7–10 minutes and squeezed to obtain the sour juice. Ready-to-use tamarind juice is now available in the supermarket.

Taro leaf stalk

This edible leaf stalk (*phueak* in Thai) belongs to a taro family of Colocasia, *Colocasia gigantea*. It is known as *batang keladi* in Malay. The stalks are porous and are delicious in gravy-type dishes. Please make sure you buy the right kind and not to forage yourself.

Turmeric (*Curcuma domestica*)

Turmeric (*khamin*) is a knobby rhizome that imparts a bright orange colour to foods. Reputed to have antiseptic and medicinal value, it can be bought fresh or powdered.

Water chesnut

A walnut-sized tuber of certain kinds of sedges/sage. Inside the dark skin is the off-white crunchy meat. Canned water chesnuts are ready-peeled and may be substituted instead of the fresh variety.

1. Dried mushrooms. 2. Kaffir lime leaves. 3. Turmeric. 4. Coriander leaves. 5. Chinese chives. 6. Screwpine leaves. 7. Taro leaf stalks. 8. Lesser ginger.
9. Lemon grass. 10. Galangal. 11. Sweet basil leaves. 12. Kaffir lime. 13. Red chillies. 13. Bird's eye chillies. 15. Green chillies. 16. Pea eggplants.

Weights & Measures

Quantities for this book are given in Metric, Imperial and American (spoon and cup) measures. Standard spoon and cup measurements used are: 1 teaspoon = 5 ml, 1 dessertspoon = 10 ml, 1 tablespoon = 15 ml, 1 cup = 250 ml. All measures are level unless otherwise stated.

LIQUID AND VOLUME MEASURES

Metric	Imperial	American
5 ml	$1/6$ fl oz	1 teaspoon
10 ml	$1/3$ fl oz	1 dessertspoon
15 ml	$1/2$ fl oz	1 tablespoon
60 ml	2 fl oz	$1/4$ cup (4 tablespoons)
85 ml	$2^1/2$ fl oz	$1/3$ cup
90 ml	3 fl oz	$3/8$ cup (6 tablespoons)
125 ml	4 fl oz	$1/2$ cup
180 ml	6 fl oz	$3/4$ cup
250 ml	8 fl oz	1 cup
300 ml	10 fl oz ($1/2$ pint)	$1^1/4$ cups
375 ml	12 fl oz	$1^1/2$ cups
435 ml	14 fl oz	$1^3/4$ cups
500 ml	16 fl oz	2 cups
625 ml	20 fl oz (1 pint)	$2^1/2$ cups
750 ml	24 fl oz ($1^1/5$ pints)	3 cups
1 litre	32 fl oz ($1^3/5$ pints)	4 cups
1.25 litres	40 fl oz (2 pints)	5 cups
1.5 litres	48 fl oz ($2^2/5$ pints)	6 cups
2.5 litres	80 fl oz (4 pints)	10 cups

DRY MEASURES

Metric	Imperial
30 grams	1 ounce
45 grams	$1^1/2$ ounces
55 grams	2 ounces
70 grams	$2^1/2$ ounces
85 grams	3 ounces
100 grams	$3^1/2$ ounces
110 grams	4 ounces
125 grams	$4^1/2$ ounces
140 grams	5 ounces
280 grams	10 ounces
450 grams	16 ounces (1 pound)
500 grams	1 pound, $1^1/2$ ounces
700 grams	$1^1/2$ pounds
800 grams	$1^3/4$ pounds
1 kilogram	2 pounds, 3 ounces
1.5 kilograms	3 pounds, $4^1/2$ ounces
2 kilograms	4 pounds, 6 ounces

LENGTH

Metric	Imperial
0.5 cm	$1/4$ inch
1 cm	$1/2$ inch
1.5 cm	$3/4$ inch
2.5 cm	1 inch

OVEN TEMPERATURE

	°C	°F	Gas Regulo
Very slow	120	250	1
Slow	150	300	2
Moderately slow	160	325	3
Moderate	180	350	4
Moderately hot	190/200	370/400	5/6
Hot	210/220	410/440	6/7
Very hot	230	450	8
Super hot	250/290	475/550	9/10